SPEEDWAY
IN WALES

A long way from Wales – this rare 1949 shot at Christchurch, New Zealand shows two top Kiwi riders who would go on to play major roles in the story of Welsh speedway. Taking the wide outside line is track record holder Mick Holland, who would become a star of the Cardiff Dragons team, while on the inside is Trevor Redmond, the man who would bring the sport to Neath.

SPEEDWAY
IN WALES

Andrew Weltch

TEMPUS

First published 2002

PUBLISHED IN THE UNITED KINGDOM BY:
Tempus Publishing Ltd
The Mill, Brimscombe Port
Stroud, Gloucestershire GL5 2QG

PUBLISHED IN THE UNITED STATES OF AMERICA BY:
Tempus Publishing Inc.
2 Cumberland Street
Charleston, SC 29401
USA

British Library Cataloguing in Publication Data.
A catalogue record for this book is available from the British Library.

ISBN 0 7524 2701 6

Typesetting and origination by Tempus Publishing.
PRINTED AND BOUND IN GREAT BRITAIN.

CONTENTS

ACKNOWLEDGEMENTS

I am particularly grateful to Dave James and Paul Jeffries, two historians of Welsh speedway, without whose generous contributions this book would not have been possible.

Many others have also helped, with information, advice, photographs and other material. I would like to thank: Brian Jarrett, Pat Redmond, Denys Jones, David Donaldson, Brian Lee, Gareth Harris, Ian Rodger, Glenn Edwards, Tim Stone, John Jarvis, Stewart Williams, Bob Radford, Hywel Lloyd, Robert Luke and Diana Beer. Thanks also go to the unknown photographers responsible for some of the older pictures, whose origins I have been unable to establish.

I must also acknowledge the various publications which provided useful sources of information, particularly *The Western Mail*, *South Wales Echo*, *Wales on Sunday*, *Speedway Star*, *Stenner's Speedway Annual*, *Speedway Researcher* and the Tempus book *Homes of British Speedway* by Robert Bamford and John Jarvis, as well as various meeting programmes.

The Millennium Stadium photograph in Chapter One is copyright Mike Patrick (www.mike-patrick.com), and the cover photograph is by Glenn Edwards.

A final word of thanks goes, as ever, to my family – Ruth, for her continuing tolerance, and Richard and Sarah, for their help with the Cardiff research.

Andrew Weltch
Cardiff
April 2002

INTRODUCTION

The history of speedway in Wales is as chequered as the flag that ends a race. Time and again, the sport has roared into the Principality, attracted huge support and then faded away like a faulty engine.

Along with its four-wheeled cousin, stock car racing, speedway is the most urban of motor sports, so it is no surprise that its presence in Wales has been centred on the industrial towns and cities of the south coast and valleys.

The origins of speedway are, like most sports, difficult to pin down. However, its arrival in Britain is generally acknowledged as the meeting at High Beech, Essex in February 1928. It was imported from Australia, although the roots of dirt-track racing, as it was often known then, probably lie in the United States. However, it is unlikely we will ever know where the very first motorcycle races on a loose-surface track took place. Wales itself may have been among the first. The earliest motor-cycle races on Pendine Sands in South West Wales were held in 1905 and continued for half a century. In 1920, *The Motor Cycle* described Pendine as 'the finest natural speedway imaginable.' The beach course must indeed have resembled a giant version of the stadium speedways that would later spring up around Britain – with mile-long straights and a hairpin bend at the end. During the late 1920s, the star performers included some of Cardiff's speedway regulars such as Nick Carter and former Isle of Man TT star Len Parker.

Throughout 1928, speedway swept through Britain, and it arrived in Wales just before that initial boom year ended: Cardiff hosted its opening meeting on Boxing Day. From there it spread to the Valleys towns of Pontypridd, Tredegar and eventually Caerphilly. The high-speed heroes of those early dirt-track days in South Wales bore names that reflected the excitement of the sport – 'Lightning' Luke, 'Whirlwind' Baker, 'Hurricane' Hampson, and others. They were frequently joined by speedway's biggest stars from throughout the UK, as well as Australia and the USA. Although Welsh speedway at this time was mainly a contest for individuals, there was a period when the Cardiff-based Wales team seemed invincible, and even won at Wembley.

Before the end of the 1930s, however, the sport had died out in Wales, and was only revived when a new Cardiff track opened in 1951 with the launch of the Dragons. The team's enormous popularity waned after a few years, and it was another decade before the sport returned to Wales. Neath lasted a single season – and part of that in exile in Cornwall –

before Newport appeared on the scene, and would become the sport's most stable home in the Principality. Newport Wasps enjoyed their ups and downs throughout the 1960s and '70s before disappearing, and they re-emerged in the 1990s with a stable-looking future. Long-track speedway took place at Prestatyn in the north and Ammanford in the West, but it was to be the twenty-first century when the sport in Wales returned to the levels it had enjoyed in the early 1930s.

In 2001, with Newport running two teams at its purpose-built arena, the sport's biggest event, the British Grand Prix, was brought to Cardiff's Millennium Stadium, drawing tens of thousands of fans from all over the speedway world. The following year, Wales gained a new venue at Carmarthen, where a Conference League side would be based for 2002.

The following pages tell the story, or rather the stories, of speedway in Wales, from its arrival at Christmas-time in 1928 right up to the 2002 season, supplemented by a brief chapter on Wales's most famous speedway son, the double world champion Freddie Williams. Apart from the brief mention of Pendine in this introduction, the book does not attempt to cover sand racing and references to grass-track racing are generally only made when there is some significance to the development of speedway itself. Nor does it recount every effort to introduce the sport in Wales – there have been several attempts in Swansea, for instance. So, this is by no means a comprehensive record of Welsh speedway, but my hope is that it provides an interesting account of the sport's early years in Wales – which, having been scarcely mentioned in print since the contemporary press reports, receive special attention – and a useful summary of events in more recent years.

Andrew Weltch
Cardiff
April 2002

1
CARDIFF

Speedway in the capital can be divided into three distinct eras at three venues. Cardiff's White City stadium hosted the first true speedway meeting in Wales on Boxing Day 1928 and continued sporadically until 1937. The sport returned in 1951 with the launch of the Cardiff Dragons team at a new track in Penarth Road, but this lasted less than three years. Most recently, since 2001 there has been the annual visit of the sport's showpiece, the British Grand Prix, to the city's magnificent Millennium Stadium.

White City

'Thrills! Thrills!' screamed the newspaper advertisements. 'A new sensation for Wales – must be seen to be believed.' The sensation in question was 'super dirt-track racing', which had swept through Britain during 1928, following its arrival from Australia. The venue was Cardiff's White City stadium at Sloper Road, an arena which had opened for greyhound racing earlier that year and which had attracted a crowd of 70,000 to a Wales-England Rugby League international only six weeks before. The date was 26 December 1928 – an odd time to introduce a sport regarded as best suited to the summer, but it was nevertheless a huge success.

The crowd hardly matched the attendance at that Rugby League game, but some 25,000 were reported to have deserted their firesides to witness this new curiosity. As far as the city's Christmas sport was concerned, dirt-track racing was eclipsed only by Cardiff City's soccer match, which drew 28,000, and was well ahead of the Rugby Union club's attendance figure of 10,000.

Cardiff had already hosted grass-track racing – Nick Carter won the 350cc event at the Arms Park on 6 October, but this was a different spectacly altogether. The meeting attracted established stars, including New Zealander Smoky Stratton and British riders from as far away as London, Manchester and Birmingham. Up to 60 South Wales hopefuls also took part, many with experience in grass-track or road racing. The

The advertisement for the first speedway meeting in Wales – the White City, Cardiff event on Boxing Day 1928.

afternoon's event saw three separate competitions. The Cardiff City Trophy consisted of eight heats leading to a final, which was won by Cliff Upham from Jack Luke. The South Wales Scratch Race and the Golden Helmet were each run over six heats and a final. The first was won by Arthur Franklyn of Manchester, ahead of Stratton, with those positions reversed in the other.

A second meeting was held on 12 January, with the press again reporting a good crowd. One local reporter was not impressed with the early heats, describing them as 'painful to watch', but the meeting really came to life with the challenge race between 'Dare Devil' Clem Beckett of Oldham, and Coventry's Arthur Jervis. The Midlander led by fully twenty yards on the first lap, but Beckett passed him with a 'wonderful broadside' as they entered the first turn on lap two. He stayed ahead until falling near the end of lap three and, although he remounted, he could not catch Jervis. The Coventry man went on to set a new standing-start record of 98.6 seconds, taking six seconds off the time set by Stratton on Boxing Day, and equating to an average speed of over 34 mph.

Races were run, as today, over four laps, and usually from a stand-ing start. When a rolling start was used, riders had to stay below 15mph until four yards from the start line, when the starter would wave them off with a white flag. The four laps, measured along a line three feet from the inside of the track, made 1,633 yards, making a lap 408 yards.

Getting ready for the start at the inaugural Cardiff meeting on Boxing Day 1928. The first speedway event in Wales attracted 25,000 spectators.

After these winter dates, the promoters, Provincial Dirt Tracks (Cardiff) Ltd and manager Jimmy Hindle took a break of two months before a third meeting on 23 March. After that, there were meetings usually twice a week – on Saturday and Wednesday – right through to the autumn.

The crowds were still flocking in – the attendance at the meeting on 30 March was estimated at 15,000, and the Wednesday 10 April event was described in the press as an 'unqualified success'. This marked the track's first floodlit meeting and included the first team event, with a challenge between Cardiff and a side from Knowle Speedway in Bristol. The home side won by a convincing 37 points to 16, having finished first in all but one of the nine heats, the only visitor to record a victory in the match being Len Parker, who had won the sidecar Isle of Man TT four years before.

South Wales riders were by now well established and many adopted suitable nicknames – though not always willingly. Jack Luke told a reporter that he preferred 'Lightning' to the alternatives of 'Lively' and even 'Lurid', which some observers had given him. If he had a choice, he said, he would rather retain the simple 'J.H.'. He did not have a choice, however, and the name 'Lightning' stuck, along with 'Champ' (Cliff) Upham, 'Hurricane' (Fred) Hampson, 'Whirlwind' (Ron) Baker and others. The riders came from well beyond the city and there were plenty of them

– a typical riders' meeting at Barry's Hotel, Cardiff in April 1929 was attended by about fifty men from all over South Wales. The race meetings were essentially individual competitions, usually with two or three trophies on offer, and track manager 'Genial' Jimmy Hindle, who also rode, was keen to encourage newcomers. Novice competitions were held for those who had never won a race, and there were time trials which would determine whether a rider qualified for appearance money – and how much.

Ronnie 'Whirlwind' Baker, from Merthyr Tydfil, emerged as one of the rising stars of the Cardiff dirt-track scene, and broke Jervis' track record by a second in a match race with Hindle on 13 April. Just four days later, he improved further on his time, clocking 95.2 seconds in another race against Hindle, to receive a huge ovation from the crowd. Welsh riders still had some catching up to do, however. That same night, Sheffield rider Arthur Sherlock made his first appearance in Cardiff and swept the board to win all three competitions – the White City Handicap, the South Wales Scratch Race and the Cardiff City Trophy. The meeting also saw a three-team inter-city competition in a single race: Luke crossed the line first, with Sherlock second and Baker third. The result saw a win for Cardiff on 12 points, with Sheffield on 9 and Bristol on 7.

Baker's rise saw him go to the top of the points championship on 20 April when he defeated the holder R.W. 'Pip' Price and thirty-three other rivals to win the Golden Helmet. Baker shot away from the start, but Price closed the gap and they were neck-and-neck for much of the last lap. As they entered the third turn for the last time, Price seemed set to retain his title, but when they crossed the line, Baker was half a wheel ahead. Baker also won the meeting's White City scratch race, although it was a less happy occasion for J.C. Williams, who suffered a fractured collarbone in an accident with Ivor Hill. Prolonged dry weather was said to be making the track hard, and more dangerous – in another incident at the same meeting, Hill performed a somersault after running into Baker's bike.

The following Wednesday saw another inter-city challenge against Bristol, and Cardiff again scored a comfortable win. Home riders won seven of the eight heats to produce a 33-14 victory. A best-of-three match race series saw Jack 'Lightning' Luke defeat Bristol challenger Len Parker 2-0, and Luke won the Golden Gauntlet to move within a point of Baker in the track championship. Points for the championship were awarded only to winners of the regular competitions, with four points for breaking the track record, three points for the Golden Helmet, the *Western Mail* Trophy or the Cardiff City Trophy, and two points for the Golden Sash or Golden Gauntlet.

The return of Arthur Sherlock on 1 May saw the 'Sheffield Flyer', as press advertisements dubbed him, fail to reproduce the all-conquering

'Pip' Price, one of the first holders of the White City Golden Helmet in 1929.

form of his first visit. However, he made light work of Luke in a best-of-three series and won the handicap race, but lost to Upham in the Cardiff City Trophy and the Flying Nine. It was a heat in this latter event which had a huge crowd enthralled. Hurricane Hampson held a slight lead over Sherlock until the last lap, when the Sheffield man snatched the lead after tearing down the straight. Hampson fought back, and recovered the lead coming out of the final turn to take a narrow but popular win.

Visits by big stars, or 'cracks' as they were then known, became a regular feature, though their appearances seldom lived up to expectation. The list of visitors in May 1929 alone (and their descriptions in the publicity) included Sheffield's George Wigfield ('who has beaten "Daredevil" Beckett'). Also featured were Australian Jack Chapman ('world mile record holder'); New Zealander Smoky Stratton ('world's champion'); Arthur Sherlock ('the Sheffield Flyer' again); 'Stewie' St George ('Australian champion' –in fact a New Zealander); Syd Parsons ('the most spectacular Australian in Europe') and Frank Duckett ('Australian record holder'). It seems the stars visiting Cardiff sometimes faced challenges away from the track too. On at least one occasion there was a raw egg-eating contest, won with ease by Jack Luke – a baker's son – with a total of 22.

Chapman made his European debut at Cardiff on 8 May and beat Hampson in the traditional match races, but he had little other success and was thrown during the final of the Whitchurch Handicap. Although he had apparently only sprained a toe, he took no further part in the meeting. Stratton, who had set the track record at the opening meeting on Boxing Day, and was described as holding six world records, made a similarly disappointing appearance when he flew into Cardiff from Sheffield and received a huge ovation from the crowd. There were even bigger cheers in heat four of the handicap competition, when Barry rider Ray 'Sunshine' Cannell defeated the visiting star. The handicap system gave the local man a full eight seconds start, which proved too much for Stratton to overcome. The New Zealander fell in a challenge race with Upham, and was said to be so badly shaken he could not take part in the other events.

Sherlock won the final of the scratch race in front of the biggest crowd of the season when he returned on 15 May, though his challenge series with Hurricane Hampson was notable for the local man taking a second off the track record. Parsons beat Champ Upham in the challenge races when he appeared on Whit Monday 20 May, but did not get in the money in the other events. The next day Sherlock returned, but was thwarted by mechanical trouble, and he made an apology to the crowd over the loud speaker system, hoping to come back soon and deliver a performance as good as his first. That meeting also witnessed a dead heat, when Baker darted inside Hampson on the final straight to share the honours in a challenge race, which replaced the abandoned contest between Sherlock and Baker.

A snapped chain, a fall, and finally a broken bike marred Duckett's visit on 25 May, but the meeting saw a new name on the Cardiff championship board when E.A. Dunlop of Bridgend beat the big names to win the Golden Sash. Four days later, there were three star guests in the White City line-up – Duckett, fellow Australian Ned Kelly and Sheffield's Sherlock. Although the Englishman won the scratch race final, Baker defeated both Australians in rolling-start match races, before dead-heating with his rival Hampson in a final challenge. In his win over

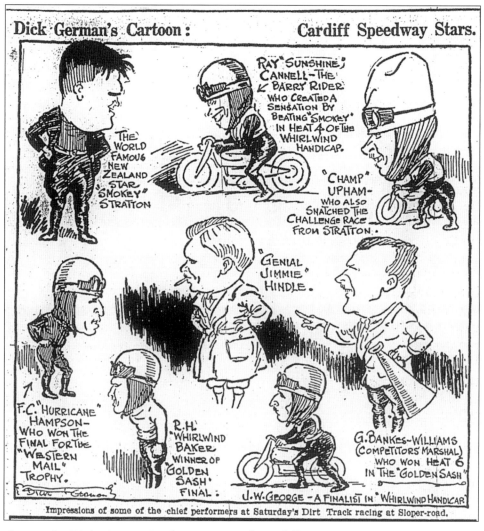

Cartoonist Dick German's observations of Cardiff's 11 May 1929 meeting, when Barry rider Ray 'Sunshine' Cannell scored a popular win.

Duckett, Baker shaved a second off the track record – which Hampson had set less than a week earlier – posting a new best time of 93.4 seconds.

While individual contests remained the principal fare for Cardiff dirt-track fans, team racing was emerging as an additional attraction. A four-man team travelled to Bristol for a return fixture, which ended in a draw. The Cardiff team comprised Champ Upham, Whirlwind Baker, Jimmy Hindle and J.W. George. Lightning Luke, surely a natural choice, missed the fixture through a racing injury which kept him sidelined for most of May 1929.

Buster Frogley brought his Wembley team to Wales on 8 June to face the strong four-man Cardiff side of Hampson, Baker, Hill and Luke. The four-heat match ended 14-14, while Frogley beat Hill 2-0 in the best-of-three challenge. A return match in London the following Tuesday saw Cardiff score a surprise 12-9 victory over Wembley. The six-man team featured Hill, Hampson, Baker, Upham, Hindle (captain) and Luke. 'Champ' Upham lived up to his name, winning the night's handicap competition. The victorious team got home to Cardiff at 5.30 the next morning, and may well have been relieved that heavy rain forced the cancellation of that night's meeting at White City.

Further reductions in the Cardiff track record saw Ivor Hill setting a new rolling start fast time of 90.2 seconds, and there was a record of

Fay Taylour's appearance drew a huge crowd to the White City. Here she lines up alongside Jack Luke, whom she faced in a series of match races.

The Cardiff-based Wales team, which scored a famous victory at Wembley in 1929. From left to right: Ivor Hill, Fred 'Hurricane' Hampson, Ron 'Whirlwind' Baker, Jimmy Hindle, 'Champ' Upham, Jack 'Lightning' Luke, and an unidentified rider.

another kind in June, when Fay Taylour became the first woman rider to appear at the White City track. Her visit was well publicised, with much made of her success at Wembley the previous week, when she had taken a second off the one-lap record in front of 40,000 spectators. Some of the programme notes for her Cardiff appearance are now quite amusing: 'An erroneous impression was created that, on account of Miss Taylour's motorcycling activities, she might be somewhat masculine. Such is not the case, as Miss Taylour is a pretty, petite English girl, whose charming smile is captivating.'

Like many of the star visitors, Taylour was out of luck at Cardiff. In front of a crowd reported to be a record for an ordinary meeting, she fell in the first of her challenge races against Jack Luke, suffering an injury which was later said to be more serious than she had admitted. She came out for the second race, but was uncompetitively slow, and took no further part in the meeting. A cartoonist at the time suggested that the mask she chose to wear might have scared Luke off at high speed.

The meeting also saw Whirlwind Baker carried off with concussion and facial injuries, after crashing badly in front of the packed grandstand after clipping a rival's wheel.

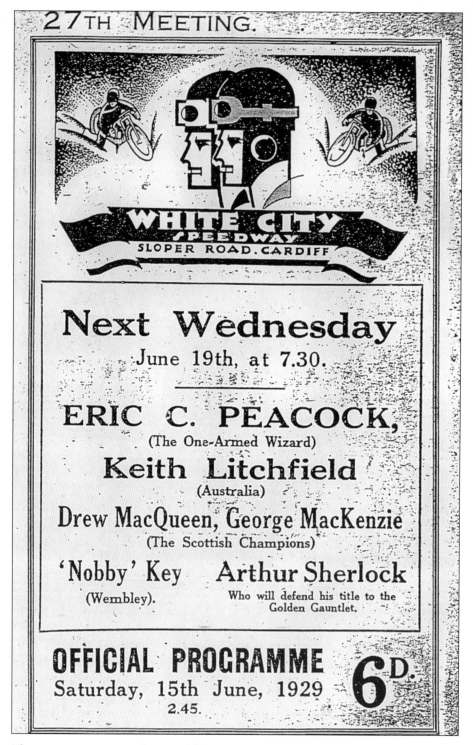

27TH MEETING.

WHITE CITY SPEEDWAY
SLOPER ROAD, CARDIFF

Next Wednesday
June 19th, at 7.30.

ERIC C. PEACOCK,
(The One-Armed Wizard)
Keith Litchfield
(Australia)
Drew MacQueen, George MacKenzie
(The Scottish Champions)
'Nobby' Key   Arthur Sherlock
(Wembley).   Who will defend his title to the Golden Gauntlet.

OFFICIAL PROGRAMME
Saturday, 15th June, 1929
2.45.
6D.

The programme cover for Cardiff's 15 June meeting, when Fay Taylour was the star attraction.

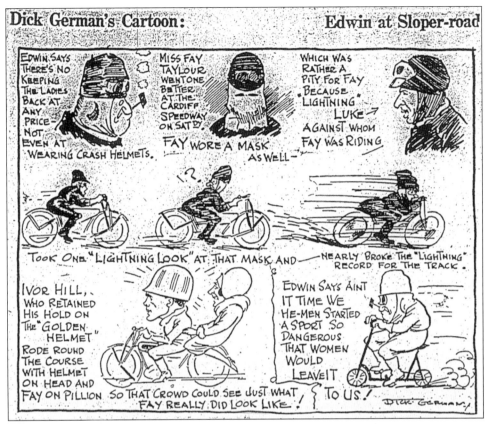

Dick German's reflections on Fay Taylour's Cardiff visit, suggesting that her mask scared Jack Luke off at speed.

Further international visitors included Scottish duo Drew MacQueen and George Mackenzie making their Welsh debuts, while Champ Upham and Hurricane Hampson made the journey in the opposite direction to compete in Edinburgh. The biggest name of all, however, was Lloyd 'Sprouts' Elder, who was booked to race at the White City on Wednesday 26 June. The legendary American was regarded as the greatest dirt-tracker of the sport's early days, and his appearance attracted a new record crowd. So many people were still outside the stadium at the scheduled 7.30 p.m. start time that the meeting was delayed. Whirlwind Baker was the man chosen to face this illustrious visitor in the customary three-race challenge, but this time the home man came off second best. Elder roared into the lead at the start of the first, and stayed ten lengths in front to win the heat in a new standing-start record time of 91 seconds. The second race, from a rolling start, saw the crowd go wild as Baker took a first-lap lead. The American got past a lap later, however, before losing his chain. Baker fell on the fourth turn of the final lap, but remounted to finish alone and set up a third-race decider. Elder made no mistake this time, again from a rolling start, beating the local star and setting another new record of 89 seconds. Champ Upham received a huge cheer for beating Australian Syd Parsons in a heat of the Cardiff City Trophy, whose final went to Nick Carter, after Elder again lost his chain.

Team racing returned on 29 June, with another challenge against Bristol. Cardiff won again, 16-13, but the meeting saw Ivor Hill break his collarbone in a bad spill in heat three, leaving him unable to defend his Golden Helmet title. That honour went to Nobby Key, who also received the £10 first prize.

The next big-name visitor was South Australian champion Charley Gray, but in the first race of the 3 July meeting against Key, he fell at the end of the second lap and suffered a broken collarbone. Baker won the Golden Gauntlet that night, becoming the first rider to win every major Cardiff trophy and taking a clear lead in the championship table. That weekend, Key faced Baker in the match races. Both beat Elder's new record, with Baker coming out on top and taking two-fifths of a second off the American's time.

The record for the slowest race was set on 10 July, when all three riders fell in the fourth heat of the Flying Twelve. Australian Dicky Wise completed the last quarter of a lap by running with his machine to finish in 140.2 seconds! The return of team racing a week later saw West Ham, representing England, face Cardiff's Wales team. The home side won 38-25, with Champ Upham rated the match's top rider. Lightning Luke sprained his ankle in a fall and had to withdraw from the meeting. The Wales team also included Hurricane Hampson, Whirlwind Baker, Nick Carter and Nobby Key. By the end of July, Cardiff had also beaten Sheffield, led by the great Smoky Stratton, 41-20, and Nottingham 20-8, in front of a crowd of 8,000.

A match against the West of England on 3 August was 'somewhat farcical' reported one journalist, because the wet track left riders with bikes clogged, and many were unable to complete the course. Wales won 17-8. There were better conditions four days later, when Midlands were the visitors. Although the Midlands' captain, Wally Lloyd, impressed, Wales won 22-5.

The great Vic Huxley was back on 10 August, and set new records for both a rolling (1 minute 26.8 seconds) and standing start (1 minute 30 seconds), before Sprouts Elder's return a week later. Elder's first match race against Baker was described as a 'fiasco', after the local hero fell on the third lap and again on the fourth, and Elder lost his chain towards the end of the last lap and had to push his bike to the finish line. The lanky American star was in such demand that his South Wales visit saw him booked in to appear at Pontypridd after his afternoon races in

Cardiff, having already competed at Tredegar the previous night (see Chapter Two).

Yorkshire heroine Eva Askquith, rated alongside Fay Taylour as head and shoulders above the other women riders of the time, defeated Jimmy Hindle in a match race series, when she visited Cardiff on 21 August – but apparently only after some chivalry by the White City rider-promoter. Askquith fell on the last lap, and Hindle dismounted to give her a push-off, which sent her away to win the deciding race.

The Cardiff-based Wales team faced its toughest challenge on 24 August when Wembley again ventured across the border. The London track's manager, the 'father of British speedway' Johnnie Hoskins, said he was sending his strongest four-man team – Jack Ormston, Ron Hieatt, Jack Barrett and Jack Jackson – in the hope of breaking the Welsh side's winning record. A local newspaper reported: 'He is of the opinion that the bunch who are coming will give the Welshmen their first defeat, and he says that if they don't, then no team ever will.' As it turned out, Wembley brought a weakened line-up and lost 17-11 to the home side.

An England-Wales match on 11 September was similarly billed as the locals' toughest test. 'This is easily the strongest team to visit Wales,' read the newspaper advertisement, but the English line-up, which included Stan and Eric Spencer, Clem Cort and Jim Kempster, was crushed 48-16. Welsh-based riders won each of the nine races, with Ron Baker, Cliff Upham and Nobby Key each scoring three victories. A week later, Salford were the visitors and Wales won 18-10.

The season ended on 4 October with a charity meeting in aid of Cardiff Royal Infirmary. Novelty events included match races between two Barry riders, F. 'Speed' Jones and C.R. Coslett – both having the reputation of never completing the four laps without falling. Coslett won the deciding race.

By any measure, Cardiff's first speedway season had been a huge success, and the riders – with their heroic nicknames – had become local celebrities. Cliff 'Champ' Upham spent some of his season's winnings on a speedboat and was reportedly seen practising broadsiding in the Bristol Channel. Both he and Ron 'Whirlwind' Baker announced they would be wintering in Australia.

There was understandable optimism as the spring of 1930 arrived. New promoters Welsh Speedways Ltd were to run the Sloper Road stadium, with Jack Lyons, a leading light in the South Wales Riders' Union, as manager. The 100 per cent home record of the Cardiff team from the previous year prompted the management to offer £200 to any team in the world, or any combination of riders who beat the Welsh at their White City home.

Billy Clibbett won the track championship race at the season opener on 2 April, and a week later he beat 'Smiling' Jim Kempster in

Dai Lossin On The Dirt Track.

OFFICIAL (to Cyclone Dai Lossin, competing at the Pontypwdyn Black City Speedway) : Here ! What do you want with a pillion-rider behind you in a dirt track race ?

CYCLONE DAI LOSSIN : Well, Jawch, mun ! If I didn't have Marget Ann behind me I'd be last ! !

More cartoon observations from early in the 1930 season, with Welsh comic character Dai Lossin.

match races, although the Londoner took the honours in the Golden Gauntlet. 16 April proved to be a disappointing night, with Stewie St George failing to appear and Hampson taken suddenly ill during a race. Fortunately, he managed to stop his machine before apparently fainting, but was allowed to go home after being attended to by ambulance men.

The first team race of the year saw Coventry visit on 19 April. Newspaper advertisements told supporters 'who live in the outside areas' that they could buy reduced-price admission tickets from rail offices and bus conductors. Wales maintained that winning record, with a 17-11 scoreline.

A Cardiff team went on to draw at Exeter, but returned to their winning ways in their next home match, a 23-5 victory over London – a team consisting of three former White City regulars, Ivor Hill, Nick Carter and Nobby Key with Del Forster. Crystal Palace were the next victims, losing 42-11 on Wednesday 7 May. The Wales team comprised consistent favourites Baker, Luke and Hampson, along with three of the year's new stars Clibbett, Ted Bravery and Pontypridd prodigy Tom Lougher.

The Palace side was led by captain Jack Barrett, who was said to regularly lap his home oval at 44mph, and included two Danish riders from Copenhagen speedway – Kai Anderson and Walthur Ryle.

Preston gave Wales their closest contest so far, the Lancashire side losing by a single point when they came to Cardiff on Wednesday 14 May. The nine-race match ended 25-24 in favour of the Welsh, although Preston's Ham Burrill was the only man to win three races. Wales finally

London line-up – the four-man London team which lost at Cardiff on 30 April 1930. From left to right: Del Forster, Ivor Hill, Nobby Key, Nick Carter. All except Forster had been White City regulars.

lost their winning record when Preston returned on 18 June. It was a great night for the visitors, with a 15-9 victory and their captain Joe Abbott breaking the Cardiff track record. However, the most exciting race of the night was the final of the Golden Sash, which saw Jack Luke hold Abbott at bay. The next night the Cardiff team went to Preston and lost again, though this time they had an excuse – they had apparently misunderstood information about the Lancashire track and the whole team rode machines that were under-geared.

Cardiff – as the team was now usually calling itself – lost at home again on 25 June, when Wembley won the four-race match 13-10, but a week later Cardiff beat visitors Portsmouth 28-26 in a nine-race contest. Despite that win, the Welsh riders had clearly lost their all-conquering touch, and this was to be the last team race of the season at the White City.

Individual competition continued, of course, but coverage in the local press was waning. The fans remained as passionate as ever, though – as they showed when local star Bill Clibbett faced visitor Ron Johnson in a

Cardiff riders form a guard of honour for Jack Luke and his bride, Josephine Hampson, sister of 'Hurricane', at Llandaff Cathedral on 26 June 1930.

match race on 4 June. Clibbett protested over the rolling start, but Johnson was allowed to complete the four laps and was declared the winner. A section of the crowd protested and after a consultation, officials ordered the race to be re-run. Clibbett fell and Johnson sportingly pulled up to allow a third attempt. On the third start, the two collided, Johnson fell and damaged the forks of his bike, finally forcing the race to be abandoned.

There were celebrations off the track on 26 June, when Jack Luke married Josephine Hampson – sister of 'Hurricane' – at the city's Llandaff Cathedral. It was a real celebrity wedding, with riders in leathers and helmets forming a guard of honour for the happy couple.

Roger Frogley won the clean-sweep of Golden Sash, Flying Nine and Cardiff City Trophy, when he visited Cardiff on 16 July, but in a brief newspaper report, the meeting of the following Wednesday was said to be 'one of the best ever run'. Ted Bravery won *The Western Mail* handicap. That best meeting also turned out to be the last of 1930, as the season at White City was curtailed.

Indeed, it was the last dirt-track racing in Cardiff for several years. It is believed there was a one-off event in 1934, although no details are known. That year also saw grass-track racing at Cardiff City's Ninian Park soccer ground, but it was not until Wednesday 21 August 1935 that speedway was re-launched at the White City. By now speedway in Britain had become firmly established as a team sport, and although Cardiff was too late to join the league that year, racing at Sloper Road would now be focused on team competition, not individuals. Improvements to the track had now made it 'probably … the fastest track in existence' according to one press preview, which also reassured spectators that new Auto Cycle Union (ACU) contracts would end the disappointments of previous years when star riders failed to appear because they had received a better offer.

More than 13,000 people welcomed speedway's return to the city, when a Colonial team beat the English Cubs 61-43 in an eighteen-heat contest. A 'local talent' race, incidentally, saw victory for Tom Lougher of Pontypridd – who had become one of the top names at the White City five years before and had gone on to ride for West Ham.

Times had changed in those few years, with rider earnings slashed. In the pioneer years, the top men in South Wales might have picked up £40 a week, whereas they were now hard-pushed to earn £10 or £15. Cardiff track manager Captain Dick Southouse, who had been a pioneer rider at Leicester and later a promoter at Coventry and Luton, said: 'Sanity has come to the finance of dirt-track riding. It is all to the good of the game.'

The following week, Cardiff's new team – assembled mainly from riders who had made their names at English tracks – made its debut against Plymouth. Norman Trimnell from Birmingham was highlighted for his unusual riding style, supporting himself on his legs rather than sitting in the saddle, and the Cardiff team also included John Deeley, who had scored maximum points for England the previous week. This time, Deeley failed to win a race, and the home team lost the nine-heat match 31-22. For the record, Cardiff's line-up was completed with Lew Lancaster, Keith Harvey, Chun Moore, Jack Dalton and Cecil De Laporte.

On 4 September, Hackney Wick were the visitors. Curiously, their side included Deeley, while Cardiff's featured old favourite Ted Bravery from Bristol – who had ridden for Plymouth the week before. The Londoners went home 28-23 winners, but the Wales-based team's first win would come a week later, against another London side, West Ham. Cardiff were just one point ahead after the seventh heat, but scored a 31-22 victory thanks to 5-1 wins in the last two races. Wembley were next to visit, but a soft track hindered the racing and doubtless favoured the home side, who romped away to a 40-14 win.

There was further success on 25 September, when Cardiff ended an eight-match winning run for Liverpool side Seaforth with a somewhat hollow 29-22 victory. The home team were 24-22 ahead going into the last heat, but both visitors fell, leaving Phil Hart and Keith Harvey to take a 5-0 heat win.

The last event of a short, seven-meeting season was the Cardiff Riders Championship on 2 October, but the contest was abandoned after six races because torrential rain had made the track dangerous.

The close-season saw considerable work on the track, with bends and straights widened by up to twenty feet and the surface almost entirely relayed with a mixture of cinder and stone dust. This prompted the familiar annual newspaper claim that 'Cardiff now possesses one of the finest and fastest tracks in the whole country'. There was particular reason for excitement as the 1936 season approached for Wales would for the first time be entering a team in league competition. Cardiff signed up for the new Provincial League, effectively a second division of the National League.

Cardiff's home matches would continue to be on a Wednesday night, and their team colours would be blue and yellow. Opponents would be Nottingham, Plymouth, Southampton, Bristol and Liverpool, with each six-man team facing each other twice at home and twice away in twelve-heat matches, in addition to a National Provincial Trophy competition, involving all the league's teams plus a reserve side from National League club West Ham. There would be no starting money, but point money at 10 shillings (50 pence) per point was reckoned to mean a top man could earn £25 a week, and a crowd of 3,000 would mean the promoters were making a profit.

Pre-season publicity announced that Cardiff's team would be captained by George O'Brien, who had moved from Luton the previous season after that track closed while he had been in hospital with a fractured skull. Also in the squad was Jack Bibby, who would miss the start of the season as he was en route from Australia, and would temporarily be replaced by relative newcomer Charles Lish. Retained from the 1935 campaign were Lew Lancaster, South African Keith Harvey and Bristol's Ted Bravery, while South Wales's home-grown talent was represented by Tom Lougher of Pontypridd and Newport man Roy Zeal.

The season began with a Good Friday visit to Southampton for the preliminary round of the trophy, when 14,000 saw the home team win 38-33. The return match on Easter Monday marked Cardiff's first appearance before their fans. O'Brien scored a maximum 12 points and recorded the fastest time of the night, but his team lost 33-37.

They lost a league match at a rainy Nottingham 38-34 on Tuesday 21 April before the first home league match against Liverpool next night. The Cardiff squad was strengthened with the inclusion of former West Ham rider Stan Dell and rising Wembley star Tommy Price, and the home side duly won 42-28. However, Southampton again proved too strong when they returned for a league encounter on 29 April and ran out 37-33 winners. Cardiff got back to winning ways when Plymouth arrived on 6 May, scoring a 37-34 victory, despite criticism that home riders were taking corners too wide and allowing the visitors room on the inside.

A combined Nottingham, Plymouth, Southampton and Liverpool team, known as 'The Rest', provided the opposition a week later. The visitors included Bibby, who had temporarily joined Plymouth, but managed only two third places, while Bravery and Price each scored 12 points to lead the home team to a 34-22 win.

After a 38-33 defeat at Bristol, Cardiff were hoping for better in the home match on 20 May. Further team changes saw the arrival of two former Wembley men, George Greenwood – who would replace O'Brien as captain – and Cliff Parkinson, in time for the clash with the league leaders from across the channel. Bravery lived up to his name, when he collided with Bristol's Harry Shepherd, was thrown over the handlebars, landed on his head and somersaulted several times. After attention from the St John Ambulance, he managed to get to the start line for the re-run within his two minutes. He ran second behind Shepherd for most of the race, until the last bend when he broke through to win. Cardiff won the match 39-32.

The following week, they lost at home to Nottingham by a single point, 33-32, after Price's machine failed to start for the last heat. The track was not helping either, with criticism of a spot which had developed on the inside of the south bend which was sometimes throwing riders who hit it. Whit Monday, 1 June, saw the visit of West

SPEEDWAY

2,000,000

SAW SPEEDWAY RACING LAST YEAR!

WERE YOU

ONE

OF THEM?

GET THE THRILL OF YOUR LIFE
ON EASTER MONDAY, 7.30, AT
WELSH WHITE CITY,
SLOPER ROAD.

"*DAILY, MAIL*" *TROPHY* :

CARDIFF *v.* SOUTHAMPTON

ADMISSION: Grand Stand 2/6; Enclosure 1/3.
COVERED STANDS ALL PARTS ,, *BUFFETS*
Trams from Station Approach.   Buses from Royal Hotel.

An advertisement for Cardiff's first home match of 1936. The season started with high expectations, but poor crowds and high running costs would see it end prematurely.

Ham Hawks in the Provincial Trophy, a match which Cardiff won 43-28, but celebrations were short-lived. By the end of the week, it was announced that the track was closing and Cardiff were withdrawing from the league. A brief newspaper report stated that the decision was due to poor public response and the heavy expense of league racing, which had combined to create substantial losses. However, further occasional racing was possible in the future.

Cardiff sportingly fulfilled one final fixture at Plymouth, where the Devonians won heavily, but it counted for nothing, as the ACU wiped Cardiff's results from the league. One report said the Welsh team's withdrawal had 'almost resulted in chaos', although the league simply continued with its five remaining teams – all of which were said to be enjoying attendance up to expectations – in some cases it was increasing every week.

Speedway made one further appearance at the Welsh White City on 24 July 1937, when Hackney Wick scored a 10-point win over a team representing the Provinces. Bravery, Dick Case, Cordy Milne and Bill Clibbett were reported to be the meeting's outstanding riders.

The stadium's owners made an unsuccessful application to enter a team in the Rugby League, before selling the site to a private company who used it as a sports ground.

Penarth Road

The National League folded for the duration of the Second World War, but re-emerged stronger than ever and the late 1940s saw speedway hit its peak of popularity. In 1946, more than six and a half million people watched the sport at thirteen tracks. The following year, it was more than nine million at

The new Penarth Road stadium opened in 1951 as home of the Cardiff Dragons.

23 tracks, in 1948 it was ten and a half million at 29 tracks, and in 1949 the 34 British tracks attracted twelve and a half million spectators.

By 1950, however, the sport was starting to lose fans and venues. Wales had missed out on speedway's glory years – the boom was over, and a long, slow decline was beginning. Unfortunately, this was the backdrop against which Cardiff's new speedway stadium opened. The story goes that the idea for bringing the sport back to Cardiff came from a Dorset man, Leslie Maidment, who overheard a Cardiff visitor to Southampton speedway complaining that the Welsh city had no track. Maidment travelled to Cardiff to put matters right, and teamed up with Major A.J. Lennox, an accomplished motor-cyclist who had been thinking along similar lines. Several sites were investigated and rejected before they found a suitable location in Penarth Road – not far from the city's original dirt track. Allotment holders had to be bought out, and within six weeks the land was levelled and ready for the track to be laid. Maidment brought in his old friend Alf Elliot, an authority on track construction, to oversee the work, and the new 400-yard Cardiff speedway was opened in October 1950.

Elliot stayed on as team manager and Cardiff Dragons joined the National League Division Three for 1951, along with two other new sides, Long Eaton and Wolverhampton. Cardiff signed Arthur Pilgrim from Exeter as captain and Australian Mick Callaghan from Bristol. The team for the opening *Daily Mail* National Trophy match at Rayleigh Rockets on 31 March also included New Zealanders Mick Holland and Kevin Hayden, Harry Hughes, Jimmy Wright, Frank Johnson and Ray Beaumont. The thirty-three-year-old Holland was Cardiff's top scorer with nine points from his six rides, as Dragons crashed to a 40-68 defeat.

Their opening home fixture was the return leg on Thursday 5 April, when an estimated 20,000 saw Holland again lead the Cardiff scoring, with 14. Fellow Kiwi, Hayden, the team's youngest rider also impressed with nine, but a 56-52 defeat meant the Welsh team were out of the competition.

Next came the Festival of Britain Trophy, a ten-a-side, twenty-heat competition, which began with a visit to Swindon on 14 April. Cardiff were placed in the Third Division's Central Zone, along with Rayleigh, Long Eaton and their first opponents, Swindon. Dragons led the first leg at the Wiltshire track until heat eighteen, but had to settle for a 60-60 tie. Holland scored another 14, and with solid support from Pilgrim (13) and Wright (12), Cardiff were starting to look a stronger outfit. Callaghan had a bad night, however, collecting just two points, and taking a nasty tumble when his front forks came adrift. 'I did not know whether to stay in the saddle or go on with the handle bars!' he said later.

The return match on 19 April drew 15,000 and featured a thrilling finish. With two heats left, the score was 54-54, but in heat nineteen,

"With Best Wishes"
Mick Holland

New Zealander Mick Holland was perhaps Cardiff Dragons' biggest star – a top import in their first season, he went on to become captain and was with them until the team folded in 1953.

Harry Hughes was left at the gate with engine trouble and Frank Johnson fell on the last bend, giving Swindon a 5-1 win to make the score 59-55 going into the nominated riders race. Wright and Hayden had to finish first and second to clinch a draw: Wright took the chequered flag, but Hayden could only manage third, giving the visitors a 61-59 win.

The Festival Trophy trail continued at Rayleigh on 21 April. Holland was back on form, with a 17-point haul, but despite a two-point lead at the interval, Dragons lost 66-54. Their first victory finally came at Penarth Road five days later, with an 83-36 demolition of Long Eaton in front of a 10,000 crowd. The win was marred, however, by a serious and spectacular accident in heat six, when Cardiff were leading 22-8. Dragons duo Callaghan and Pilgrim were leading, when Long Eaton's Bob Ibbotson hit the wall and fell on to the track. Unable to avoid his team-mate, Fred Siggins hit the stranded rider and was thrown six feet into the air for a distance of thirty or forty feet. Both were taken to hospital, where Ibbotson was treated for multiple fractures of the skull, broken collarbone, ribs, hip and pelvis, and Siggins for a broken leg. The visiting team also included Percy Brine, who had ridden regularly at the old Sloper Road track. He scored four points and fascinated the crowd with a demonstration of the old-fashioned, leg-trailing style of riding.

A visit to Wolverhampton ended in a 45-39 defeat, with Holland the only man in double figures with 12 points, but it was a happier story for Rayleigh's return on 3 May. A thrilling end to the match saw Cardiff pull back a two-point deficit going into the final, nominated riders', heat. Holland finished ahead of Pilgrim to give Dragons a 5-1 heat win and a 61-59 victory on the night. Rayleigh won the Festival match on aggregate, however, thanks to their bigger win at home.

A week later, international speedway returned to Cardiff, when the USA beat a West of England team, led by Rayleigh's Jack Unstead and Aldershot's Trevor Redmond, 46-38 in a fourteen-heat match in front of 15,000 fans. That same night, Cardiff were in Festival Trophy action at Long Eaton in a match they lost 58-62.

Dragons opened their league campaign with a disappointing 33-51 defeat at Plymouth on 14 May, but bounced back to score a 48-36 win over the Americans in Cardiff three days later. Holland and Wright topped the scoring list with 11 each, but the most encouraging sign of the evening was the performance of young reserve Ray Beaumont (who had regained his place in the side after Vic Butcher fractured his wrist) and ended the night with seven points.

Three successive away league defeats followed in the space of four days, with scores of 28-55 at Aldershot, 32-52 at Exeter and 41-43 at St Austell. Cardiff were not helped by a foot injury to Callaghan, which saw the Australian riding with stitches in the wound for some time. When the

Dragons' first league victory came, it was a big one – the 50-31 home win over St Austell was witnessed by a crowd of 12,000.

The stars of the Cardiff team had now started to emerge, and the final riders' averages in the Festival of Britain Trophy showed Holland and Wright in the top 10, the former placing second in the table with an average of 14.8. However, Holland's fall in the world championship qualifying round at Cardiff on 31 May would cost his team mate a chance of first place in the competition. The meeting drew the biggest crowd since the opening night, and they eagerly anticipated the heat involving Wright, Holland, Coventry's Derek Tailby, who had won his three previous races, and Wolverhampton's Vic Sage. Holland fell on the first bend, and Wright established a comfortable lead, but as they swept into lap two, the race was stopped because Holland's bike had not been fully cleared from the track. The race was re-run without Holland, Sage dropped out with engine trouble and Wright and Tailby were left to battle it out. The lead changed hands three times, until Wright making a supreme effort on the last lap, slid and fell, leaving Tailby a clean run home. The Coventry man went on to win his remaining race to take a 15-point maximum and the winner's cheque.

Despite Wright's disappointment, it was a good night for Cardiff riders, with five in the top eight – Wright was second with 13, Holland fourth with 11, Callaghan fifth on 10, Pilgrim equal sixth with 9 points and Hayden eighth with 8.

Meanwhile, grass-track racing – the 'country cousin' of speedway – continued to be popular in Wales, and even ventured into the city occasionally. The Welsh championships were held at Cardiff's Sophia Gardens in June, attracting a crowd of some 5,000. Roger Wise of Bristol won the title, which was not defended by the 1950 champion – and now a Cardiff Dragon – Vic Brinkworth.

A 53-31 home defeat by Aldershot in a challenge match on 7 June was followed two days later by a 48-36 league win over Plymouth. Mick Callaghan's form was improving, as was young Gerald Pugh's – the former grass-tracker from Hereford in his first season of speedway. Less encouraging was the attendance of 8,000 – a healthy total by most standards, but the first time the Penarth Road crowd had dropped below five figures.

Heavy defeats at Long Eaton (32-52) on Thursday 14 June and Wolverhampton (30-54) the next night were followed by a superb 59-25 win over Long Eaton on Saturday 16 June. The match was marred, however, by an accident involving Callaghan, which saw the Australian clip Hayden's rear wheel and crash into a lamp standard. His leg was broken above and below the knee and his shoulder dislocated.

A 42-42 tie at home to Swindon was followed by a 52-30 challenge win over a combined Oxford and Poole team, but in late June the club was

Australian Mick Callaghan was one of the heroes of Dragons' early days, but suffered a broken leg and dislocated shoulder in a fall in June 1951.

Gerald Pugh was hailed as a promising youngster in the 1951 campaign and was a leading scorer the following year, helping Cardiff to a second place finish in the Southern League.

facing something of an injury crisis, with five riders – Callaghan, Rob Hyde, Vic Butcher, Harry Hughes and Roy Bartlett – sidelined with injury. A supporters' collection raised £53 to help them, and there were ambitious plans to raise enough money to send Callaghan back home to convalesce.

On 28 June Dragons lost at home 44-40 to Rayleigh and added to that injury list, when Jimmy Wright was taken to hospital with a shoulder injury which was expected to keep him out of action for several weeks. The match saw Pugh's rise continue – he led the Cardiff scoring with 10. That result sparked a run of six successive league defeats, which only ended with a 41-41 draw at Wolverhampton on a date which proved unlucky for the Wasps, Friday 13 July. Indeed, Dragons looked set for a win as the last heat started. Pugh raced away, confident of securing a maximum, but he fell on the last lap, causing a pile-up, which resulted in Wasps' Harry Wardropper being stretchered off. He recovered to join the restart, from which Pugh was excluded, but this time the home team's Jack Cunningham crashed and was ruled out of the second restart. Wardropper beat Holland in the two-man race to level the match.

Injuries and that run of bad results, led to new signings. Charlie May arrived from Southampton for what was reported to be a record fee for a Third Division transfer, and Wal Morton came from non-league Ipswich. May made his home debut in a 55-29 win over Long Eaton on 14 July. The result ended a run of eight league matches without a victory, and saw three men miss out on a maximum by just one point – Pugh, Hayden and new man May all scoring 11 points. There was still a lot of work to be done, however, with Cardiff ninth in the 10-team division.

A 52-25 home win over bottom-placed Wolverhampton was no more than expected, although the meeting was notable for the first Cardiff maximum in a league match – Kevin Hayden scoring 12, with Charlie May and Gerald Pugh both contributing 11. Heavy defeats at Poole and Plymouth followed, before two narrow home wins, both 43-41, over Plymouth and Exeter.

A break in league action on 7 August saw Cardiff host another international match, when England C (a team drawn from the Third Division) beat New Zealand 55-53. Dragons' Charlie May led the England scoring with 14, while two other Cardiff men, Holland and Hayden, featured in the Kiwis' line-up. The most impressive rider of the night, however, was Trevor Redmond, the Aldershot man, who led the New Zealand scoring with 12 points from six starts, despite pulling out of one race with a flat tyre. Redmond, a riding partner with Holland back home, would play a key role in the story of Welsh speedway a decade later, when he set up a new Dragons team in Neath (see Chapter Two).

Two days later, Redmond was back in Cardiff with Aldershot Shots and scored a maximum 12, although his side went down 48-36. Pugh was

The programme cover for the visit of Aldershot, a match which Cardiff won 48-36.

now establishing himself as one of Cardiff's top men and, alongside Wembley's Welshman Eric Williams, won a best pairs competition at Odsal. Another new name was emerging in the Dragons' line-up, Chum Taylor – a young Australian who arrived on loan from Glasgow Ashfield and immediately showed great promise, as demonstrated by his five points from two rides in a home draw with Swindon on 16 August.

A solid run-in to the end of the season included huge home wins over struggling Wolverhampton (65-19) on 30 August and St Austell (66-18) on 6 September, and the final home league match saw a 45-39 win over Rayleigh, with Pugh recording his second successive maximum 12. Vic Brinkworth and Arthur Doughty were brought in at reserve, allowing Les Moore and Frank Johnson to ride first string. Dragons ended the season a respectable seventh, having won 13, lost 3 and drawn 2 of their 18 home matches and managing a single draw from their 18 away trips.

Australian Aub Lawson, a star of First Division West Ham, guested for Cardiff in a late-season challenge match against Bristol, who had finished sixth in the top flight. He and Pugh scored maximums in a 48-35 win, but Holland and Hayden were involved in a major tangle, which left the latter with his right arm broken in two places and his left arm so badly bruised that it too had to be encased in plaster.

An international pairs competition featured riders from all three divisions, representing six countries – Wales, England, Scotland, New Zealand, Australia and Canada. The Welsh pair of Pugh and Swindon's Bob Jones pipped England A's Cardiff duo Charlie May and Arthur Pilgrim in a run-off, after they had tied at 25 points each. The season ended with Penarth Road hosting the Third Division riders' championship, which was won by Poole's Ken Middleditch, with Dragons' Mick Holland the top home man down in tenth place.

During the winter, the Third Division promoters – all based in the South of England, the Midlands or, in Cardiff's case, South Wales – decided to re-form as the Southern League. Invitations to some Division Two teams were rejected, so the new competition was launched with the Division Three teams from 1951, except champions Poole who had moved up to Division Two, and with the addition of Ipswich and Southampton.

Dragons, now under the managership of Bill Dutton, started the season well and progressed through the first two rounds of the *Daily Mail* National Trophy, with convincing wins over Southampton and Swindon, before facing Rayleigh in the semi-final. Although Mick Holland (13 points) and Frank Johnson (11) performed well in the first leg in Essex, nobody else managed to score more than four, and the final score of 70-38 left Cardiff with a mountain to climb for the return match on 8 May. A crowd of 10,000 turned out to see the decider, but there were troubles from the start, as Frank Johnson suffered a broken ankle in a fall

Supporters' souvenirs included commemorative badges like this, marking Dragons' only two completed seasons.

in heat one, and Holland failed to reproduce his away form – scoring a single point from his first four rides. Skipper Charlie May led the way with 16 points, with Gerald Pugh and new Australian signing Hugh Geddes scoring 12 each, but the 59-48 victory was not enough to prevent the Rockets reaching the final.

Rayleigh were the team of the year in 1952, and their visits to Cardiff were exciting affairs. The league clash at Penarth Road on 22 May was another of those meetings described as the most exciting ever staged at the stadium. The 10,000 crowd was said to be so entranced at the end of the match that they did not want to go home – there was not the usual rush to the waiting buses. Cardiff won 46-38, with Holland back on form with 11 points and Australian Chum Taylor on 10. Rockets' second league visit attracted more than 12,000 and saw Dragons take a convincing 53-31 victory. Rayleigh went on to win the Southern League, with Cardiff runners-up. Of their 36 league matches that season, Rockets lost just eight, and two of them were at Cardiff.

New Zealander Kevin Hayden returned in May, after a long absence from his injury the previous season, but took a long time to return to form, and it was Charlie May who proved most consistent, ending the season with an average of 7.8 points. Pugh returned a figure of 7.4, with

Southern League runners up in 1952, from left to right, back row: Bert Edwards, Kevin Hayden, Mick Holland, Cyril Maidment (manager), Chum Taylor, Gerald Pugh. Front row: Charlie May, Hugh Geddes, Jimmy Wright.

Geddes and Holland equal on 7.2.

Cardiff ended the inaugural Southern League season with a 100 per cent home record, and some high-scoring victories, including two crushing defeats of Wolverhampton – who were considerably stronger than the old Third Division outfit. Wasps ran second in the league for a while and ended up in fourth place, though their visits to Penarth Road ended with them on the wrong side of 66-18 and 66-17 scorelines. 12 September saw another big win, 65-19 over Exeter Falcons. Although Taylor and May led the scoring with 12 each, Johnson was the star of the show –riding as second reserve, he won both his heats to stake a claim for a return to the first string.

International interest in 1952 came with the visit of touring Sweden, who faced England C (picked from Southern League riders) at Penarth Road. The Swedes won 56-52, but the three Dragons in the England team led the scoring, with May on 14, Pugh 12 and Bert Edwards, who had signed from Aldershot, 6.

Dragons' second season was certainly a satisfying one. As well as finishing second in the league, Cardiff riders had the greatest total of bonus points, and of the fourteen men used during the season, no fewer than six ended with an average of more than six points per match. Crowds were still regularly in five figures, and averaged 9,000, but the Government's entertainment tax was taking its toll on the sport, and Long Eaton failed to finish the season.

The Swedes returned at the start of the 1953 season, but their visit to Cardiff on 9 April was a bittersweet one for Dragons fans. It was another chance to see the exciting Scandinavians in action, but they were far too strong for Cardiff, who suffered a 75-32 defeat – the heaviest ever at Penarth Road. Chum Taylor raised a huge cheer from the disappointing 5,000 who braved the cold wind, when he beat world finalist Dan Forsberg to the line to set a new track record of 68.4 seconds. However, this was to be the Australian's final appearance in Dragons colours, as he was due to join First Division Bristol Bulldogs.

Early-season form was encouraging, not least an 80-28 destruction of St Austell Gulls in the National Trophy first round on 23 April, which saw Geddes, Jimmy Wright, May and Holland all in double figures from their six rides. However, the fans were not turning out in the numbers they used to. A week later, just 2,000 saw Geddes and May lead the way in a 53-31 win over Plymouth Devils. By June, the local press was calling on the club's management to take action to revive flagging interest. Geddes scored his first league maximum in a 57-27 win over St Austell on 4 June, but uncertainty over what would be happening at the next week's meeting was not inspiring confidence.

That next meeting turned out to be the track's best pairs competition – a contest won by Jimmy Wright and Frank Johnson. The meeting,

Australian Chum Taylor proved a valuable acquisition for the 1952 campaign, having made his first appearance on loan from Glasgow Ashfield the previous year. He moved to Bristol early in 1953, breaking the track record in his final appearance against Sweden.

By the end of April 1953, the press was reporting concerns about attendance. The fears were well-founded.

witnessed by a crowd of 3,000, brought Mick Callaghan, a favourite from Dragons' debut season, back to the limelight. Unable to secure a first string place this season, he partnered fellow Aussie Chum Taylor to fourth place. New Zealand pair, Mick Holland, the new Cardiff skipper, and Kevin Hayden placed second.

Cardiff completed the double over Southampton Saints with a 58-26 win on 18 June, but a new attraction of adding big-name riders to the second half of the programme got off to a disappointing start. Bristol's Jack Unstead, standing in for Wimbledon's Geoff Mardon, lost all three of his match races to Cardiff men.

Bryn Thomas had now taken over as manager, and crowds were showing signs of recovery, rising from

Speedway

Attendances Worry At Stadium

WHEN speedway racing re-appeared in South Wales in April, 1951, some 20,000 spectators filled the new Penarth - road Speedway Stadium to give it a great send-off, but this season, for five home matches, the aggregate "gate" has been below 25,000, pointing, as it were, to a speedway "slump" there when everything was going so well.

Speedway cannot be expected to pay its way with such meagre attendances as last night's 2,000, particularly as top-line team Plymouth are one of the big attractions of the Southern League.

an all-time-low of 1,800 on 11 June to 3,700 by the end of that month. A challenge match against Second Division Poole on 25 June proved a big attraction. Bert Edwards led the scoring with 10 points, as Cardiff scored a morale-boosting 43-41 win, and three days later a 47-37 victory at Swindon saw Holland lead the way with 11. The Cardiff captain had prepared for the Swindon match in an unexpected way. Practising alone at Penarth Road on the Friday, he was alarmed to see the stadium watch dog had broken loose and was heading towards him. Holland reportedly rode 15 laps at full throttle before the German shepherd gave up the chase!

The Coronation Best Pairs series came to Cardiff on 2 July, attracting a crowd of 5,000. The Cardiff duo of Holland and Geddes won the contest, putting them just five points behind series leaders Goog Hoskin and Don Hardy of Exeter, with two rounds left.

In his programme notes for the meeting, Thomas wrote: 'It is gratifying to see the crowd improving each week; in fact the numbers have doubled during the last three weeks. With the racing our boys are now serving up, it should not be long before the banks are full again.' Things must have looked different in the cold light of day, for Friday's newspapers carried the news that the club was being wound up because of high running costs and lack of support. Attendance had averaged less than 3,000, compared with 9,000 in 1952. Speedway could not compete with other sports, which cost less to put on, Thomas told reporters. If the team had gained promotion the previous season, they might have survived, he said. They hadn't and they didn't. The stadium remained derelict for many years until being built upon in 1969, but is commemorated in the name of Stadium Close, one of the roads built on the site. The capital had again lost speedway, and this time it would be almost half a century before it returned.

Millennium Stadium

A few hours before the 2000 British Grand Prix at Coventry, speedway fans received a shock. It was announced that the next British GP would be held in Wales – not at a speedway stadium but in the state-of-the-art, 72,000-seat Millennium Stadium, built for the 1999 Rugby Union world cup, home of Wales's national rugby and soccer teams. There were plenty of eyebrows raised and shaking of heads.

The international Grand Prix series had been introduced in 1995, as a new format for the world championship. Hackney staged the first British round, with Bradford holding the 1996 event, and Coventry the next three.

Moving the show to Cardiff meant a huge investment and gamble for the organisers, Benfield Sports International. It was reckoned to cost £500,000 to install the temporary track, an operation masterminded by former world champion Ole Olsen, and a crowd considerably bigger than those at previous British GPs would be needed to off-set the costs and to look respectable in the vast arena. Sections of the pitch were removed on 4,000 pallets to allow the track and safety fence to be installed. This meant bringing in some 1,800 tonnes of shale and 100 tonnes of clay. With the rows of seats nearest the front out of commission for safety reasons, the estimated 31,000 crowd didn't make the stadium look too empty.

The star-studded international line-up which entered the roofed stadium on 9 June was without doubt the most impressive ever to appear in Wales. Tony Rickardsson, of Poole Pirates and Sweden, was victorious on the night – a step on the road to the 2001 world title. Jason Crump, of Kings Lynn and Australia was second, with Poland's Tomasz Gollob third. The event was hailed as a terrific success for the sport, and the riders were quick to add their praise.

Big-time speedway comes to Wales – Tony Rikardsson leads the Grand Prix final at the Millennium Stadium on 9 June 2001, on his way to the world title.

Californian Praises Big Race in Wales

Speedway Bikes   **by Andrew Weltch**

Cardiff, Wales, Great Britain, June 9…California's former world champion Greg Hancock said competing before a 31,000 crowd sent a chill up his spine.

The 31 year old Whittier, CA born rider, was speaking after the British Speedway Grand Prix here Saturday night, the first motor sport event to be staged in the magnificent Millennium Stadium, Cardiff. Hancock and fellow Californian Billy Hamill, of Arcadia, CA, had disappointing nights on the temporary track for Britain's round of the 2001 world championship series, but nobody doubted the event had been a huge success for the sport of speedway.

Sweden's Tony Rickardsson won the Egg-sponsored Grand Prix and announced it was one of the greatest experiences of his life.

Australian Jason Crump was second, with Tomasz Gollob of Poland placing third to maintain his lead in the championship standings by two points. However, Rickardsson, riding with broken bones in his right hand, was delighted after clinching victory under the roof of the 72,500 seat stadium in downtown Cardiff.

"The atmosphere out there was fantastic," said Rickardsson. "Racing in front of a huge crowd in such a stadium was an unbelievable experience for all of us." However, organizers said the real winners were the speedway fans who witnessed the most spectacular and exciting speedway event in Britain for two decades.

There were those who doubted whether speedway could be staged in the Millennium Stadium, a venue built two years ago for the rugby world cup and also used for international soccer.

The Grand Prix was declared a huge success by everyone involved, and the crowd of more than 31,000 went home very impressed.

Defending World Champion, Britain's Mark Loram, had another mixed night. He fought through to the main event but a fall in heat 18, while chasing Jimmy Nilsen and Todd Wiltshire, left him with just eight points to add to the six he scored at the first round in Berlin.

World number two Billy Hamill fared even worse. The only rider to crash in practice, Hamill did it again in heat nine and was eliminated. Gollob now has 41 points, two more than Rickardsson with Todd Wiltshire, third on 28.

Crump said: "It was unbelievable to come out and look up at the crowd. It is the sort of thing you dream about when you are 14 or 15 years old, to come and race speedway in a stadium this full.

The first Cardiff Grand Prix was covered by media around the world. This report, by the author, appeared in the American motor sports weekly Racing Wheels.

'The atmosphere out there was fantastic,' said Rickardsson. 'Racing in front of a huge crowd in such a stadium was an unbelievable experience for all of us.' Crump praised the organisers for taking the sport to such an arena. 'It is great for the sport,' he said. 'Speedway was the real winner on Saturday night.'

Despite the lack of Welsh riders on the Grand Prix tour, there were plenty of locals among the cosmopolitan crowd. John Postlethwaite, chief executive of organisers, Benfield Sports International, was quoted in *The Western Mail* as praising the stadium as the best in Europe and the Welsh capital as an ideal location. 'We want to make it the spiritual home of speedway in the UK,' he said.

Sharing a venue with soccer's FA Cup final and other major events helped the image of speedway. Among speedway fans, the event raised the profile of Wales to heights it had not reached since its most famous racing son, Freddie Williams, won two world titles in the 1950s (see Chapter Six). The meeting was televised and reported worldwide, giving Cardiff speedway the kind of audience the Dragons could only have dreamed about.

Later that year, Postlethwaite enthused about the event in a press release announcing ticket availability for the 2002 Grand Prix. 'Judging by the public and media reaction we had after the event, we're anticipating a full house next year which will make it the second largest motorsport event in Britain next year after the Formula 1 Grand Prix at Silverstone,' he announced. The organisers of the Rally of Great Britain, also hosted in Cardiff, might have questioned that deduction, but there was no disputing that this was a major event for the sport. Postlethwaite concluded: 'The huge anticipation and demand for the date of next year's event has forced us to announce the date before this year's championship has been decided. We're all looking forward to returning to Cardiff.'

2

THE VALLEYS

Four venues in four towns have brought speedway to the South Wales Valleys, though sadly none lasted long. The sport's initial boom in the late 1920s and early '30s saw it spread from Cardiff to Pontypridd, then Tredegar and eventually Caerphilly. The Valleys did not host speedway again for another thirty years, when Neath entered the Provincial League in 1962 – a brave but ill-fated venture, which lasted for a single interrupted season.

Pontypridd

Hot on the heels of Cardiff's initial speedway venture came Pontypridd, which staged its first meeting at Taff Vale Park on Monday 20 May 1929. Thousands of tons of ashes, sifted six times, were used to construct the six-inch deep cinder track of 440 yards. The plan was for races every Saturday through the summer, and if a success, the track would be 'electrically illuminated' to allow racing to continue in the winter.

Speedway in Pontypridd was the brainchild of Mr J.E. Brooks, a local tobacconist, who had been involved in various ventures at Taff Vale over the previous ten years. When the town's Rugby League team folded in 1928, the stadium passed to Brooks, and he looked for a new sport to promote. Speedway was making headlines and Brooks went to Wembley to get some expert advice on how to proceed. The first meeting on what was publicised as 'Wales' best track' saw Cardiff take on a Valleys team in a nine-heat contest, which ended 26-26. Merthyr's Ron Baker, who had led the Valleys, set the track record of 99.8 seconds, but finished second to Cardiff's Fred (Hurricane) Hampson in the Taff Vale Scratch Race. The next Saturday night, Baker twice suffered a broken chain, but went on to win the Pontypridd Scratch Race and retain the track record.

Wembley duo Nobby Key and Australian Syd Parsons added some spice to the 1 June meeting, but the Welshmen held sway, Key's second in the Lonsdale Scratch Race behind 'Hurricane' Hampson being the visitors' only honour. Baker again won the (Tonypandy) Scratch Race and Swansea's George Gregor had victory in the Treforest Handicap.

Pontypridd's teenage sensation of 1929, Tom Lougher smiles aboard his Douglas.

An experimental midweek meeting on Thursday 6 June featured the unusual supporting attraction of a boxing exhibition by local hero Frank Moody, who took on two sparring partners in three-round bouts in a ring in front of the grandstand, as part of his build-up to a big fight in Manchester. Moody was, in fact, a co-promoter of the speedway, with Brooks, who was also chairman of the Welsh Boxing Association. On the track, Parsons beat Baker 2-0 in a series of match races and shaved 0.4 seconds off the Welshman's track record on the way, setting a new fastest time of 99.4 seconds. Nick Carter of Brynmawr won the Powderhall Handicap Race, while Ivor Hill won the Rhondda Scratch Race.

Heavy rain for the 15 June meeting prompted Brooks to allow all spectators into the grandstand, even if they had not paid the extra charge, and it was announced he was actively encouraging local talent by running practice sessions from 5 p.m. to 7 p.m. every Tuesday, Wednesday and Thursday. The Gandon Handicap went to Gregor and the Moody Scratch Race to Cardiff star 'Champ' Upham.

A week later, Pontypridd was the unlikely venue for a world-class showdown between two of Australia's greats, Syd Parsons and Jack Chapman – billed as the 'world's record holder' and second only to American legend Sprouts Elder. The two Aussies were said to be stylistic opposites, with Chapman favouring the outside line and sweeping past opponents almost effortlessly and Parsons hugging the grass to keep the inside line. The latter's tactics appear to have paid off, as he won the rolling start challenge, but it was Valleys rider Nick Carter who took home a £3 bonus for breaking the track record with a time of 98.2 seconds.

On 29 June, Londoner Nobby Key beat Ron 'Whirlwind' Baker 2-0 in the match races, and came within 0.4 seconds of Carter's record. Key also won the Dragon Scratch Race, while Y. Davies of Bridgend took the honours in the Ynys Handicap, thanks to an eight-yard handicap advantage. The following week, Davies again won the handicap, while Hampson won the Great Western Scratch Race.

Two of the Valleys' rising stars featured in the match races on 20 July – C. Phillpotts of Newbridge and seventeen-year-old Tom Lougher of Pontypridd. Honours were shared after the first two races, but Lougher was unable to start his machine for the decider. Nick Carter lent him his bike, but the local lad finished half a lap behind Phillpotts. However, Lougher won the Garth Handicap Race and would very soon go on to greater things. Unusually, the meeting saw two dead heats, both involving Swansea's George Gregor. He tied with Darran John, a product of Taff Vale Park who had sensationally won a race at Cardiff earlier in the day, and with young Lougher, whose performance that night attracted universal praise. Cardiff track manager Jimmy Hindle said: 'There is a most promising career open to this newcomer in the cinder world. His first appearance astounded everyone and utterly confounded their hand-icappers, and if he continues he will be worthy to be one of the most eminent Welsh broadsiders.'

The following week, the final of the Cambria Dash provided a sensa-tional finish, when all four riders were involved in a crash. Philpotts had to be prevented from restarting by the doctor, and Jack 'Lightning' Luke went on to win, ahead of Nobby Key. Meanwhile, attempts on the track record by Bristol's Len Parker and American Red Murch were unsuc-cessful.

Team racing returned on Thursday 1 August, when Bristol faced the home 'Valleys' team – really a more broadly-based South Wales side, featuring Hampson and Luke from Cardiff, Gregor from Swansea and local hero Lougher. The visitors won 16-5, but Lougher had a great night, winning a triangular challenge against local rivals D. Morgan of Caerphilly and D. Jones of Pontypridd and taking the honours in the Craig-y-Don Handicap. The previous day, Lougher had won the Golden Gauntlet at Cardiff's White City Stadium, having already taken the Rhiwbina Handicap there two weeks before.

A big crowd for the Bank Holiday Monday meeting on 5 August saw Y. Davies win the Holiday Handicap, G. Spalding the Flying Twelve and Champ Upham the August Scratch Race. The following Saturday, Bristol visitor Len Parker set a new record for a rolling start, as well as winning the Taff handicap and Rhondda Scratch Race. The only other event, the Cynon Handicap, went to Ron Barker. Local hero Lougher fell twice during the night, the second time injuring his back and having to withdraw from the meeting.

On 17 August, the sport's biggest name – and at six feet three inches probably its biggest rider – Sprouts Elder came to Pontypridd. Engine trouble helped ensure he lost to Nobby Key in a three-race series, although the second of their clashes was a thrilling neck-and-neck affair, which Key eventually won by two lengths. Elder went on to take the appropriately-titled Sprouts Scratch Race, however, finishing ahead of Jack Luke and Nick Carter.

A week later, team racing was back on the programme, this time with the home side racing as Rhondda, against visitors Wembley, who won 16-12. Pontypridd teenager Tom Lougher had another good night, winning two heats and coming third and second in the finals of the Ulster Handicap and Schneider Scratch Race.

Ron Baker finished inches ahead of Len Parker in the second of their match races on 31 August to take the contest 2-0, breaking the standing-start lap record in the process and earning a £50 prize from promoter Brooks. Stan Longney of Sully, starting off a six-second advantage, scored

Stan 'Broncho' Longney, one of the early Cardiff riders, became a Pontypridd regular and won the Gordon Lennox Handicap on 31 August 1929.

One Penny

TAFF VALE PARK
Speedway

Saturday September 14th, 1929.

FLYING TWELVE
(All Scratch Riders)

Baker	Luke	Upham	Price
Hampson	Parker	Douglas	Gregor
Carter	Hill	Wade	Clibbett

HANDICAP RACE - SCRATCH RACE.

ALSO THE FOLLOWING RIDERS,

| John | Lougher | Aplin | Watkins |
| Fowler | Longney | Dunlop | Lyons |

NOTE CHANGE IN TIME OF START.

Gates Open 3 - 30.   First Race 5 - 30.

Admission - Boys 6d. Ground 1/2. Stand 2/4.
(INCLUDING TAX.)
Unemployed must show cards stamped (9th week.)

The press advertisement for Pontypridd's eighteenth and final meeting.

Tom Lougher displays some of his trophies. After his home town track had closed, he enjoyed more success at Cardiff and was a member of the 1936 Provincial League team.

a rare win in the Gordon Lennox Handicap, while Parker won the Fowler Scratch Race. Pontypridd honour was upheld on 9 September when P. Watkins won the Glamorgan Handicap, while Upham won the Monmouthshire Scratch Race from a rolling start and Baker the standing-start Breconshire Scratch Race.

The season ended on Saturday 14 September, when the main event was the final of the Buick Scratch Race. Parker got his revenge for missing out in the recent match races by finishing ahead of Baker, with Lougher third. Parker also won the Flying Twelve race, while Pontypridd's own Glyn John took the Flat Handicap. By now, after 18 meetings, some local people were voicing their objections to the noise and smoke from the bikes, and crowds had waned. Although there are suggestions that there may have been one or two meetings in 1930, there seems to be no evidence to support the claims.

Grass track meetings, organised by Pontypridd and District Motorcycle Club, were held a few years later and again in the mid-1940s, but speedway proper never returned, and in 1931 the stadium was sold to the local education authority, which still owns it today.

The demise of Taff Vale Park did not, however, mean the end of Pontypridd's speedway connection. Tom Lougher continued to uphold the town's honour on the dirt-track scene. He won the Golden Sash Handicap at Cardiff on 18 September 1929 and was a member of the Wales team which met Coventry at the same venue on 19 April 1930. He later rode for Cardiff's Provincial League team in 1936 and also appeared for West Ham.

Tredegar

Within weeks of Pontypridd's opening came news that Tredegar was to become speedway's first home in Monmouthshire. W. Edgar Jones was the man behind the £600 project, which would create a track around the rugby football pitch and taking in part of the 'Association' (soccer) ground – which meant football was abandoned for the coming season. Cardiff's manager Jimmy Hindle was consulted on the design and was said to be very impressed.

The outside of the track was 504 yards and the inside 432, giving spectators in the rugby grandstand a prime view, with the winning post immediately in front of them. The track itself consisted of six inches of clinker ballast, with a facing of three inches of coke breeze – a construction described as ideal by 'experts in the sport'. It was twenty-five feet wide on the straight, forty feet wide on the bends, and was surrounded by a four-foot-high oak fence.

TREDEGAR SPEEDWAY.

FRIDAY, AUG. 16th,
At 6.30 p.m.

SPROUTS ELDER

(The World's Champion
Dirt Track Rider),

And many other English and
Welsh Stars will appear.

COME AND VISIT THE FINEST TRACK IN THE COUNTRY.

An advertisement for Tredegar's second meeting, featuring the great Sprouts Elder.

The Tredegar dirt track, predictably said to be 'the finest in Wales and Monmouthshire,' opened on Bank Holiday Tuesday, 6 August 1929. Many of the riders who had raced at Cardiff the day before made the trip to the new venue, and Hindle performed a demonstration before the races. Among the crowd of 6,800 was the local MP – one Aneurin Bevan, who as Health Minister in Labour's post-war government would found the National Health Service some nineteen years later. Nick Carter, from nearby Brynmawr, won the Recreation Ground Handicap and set the best time of the day.

The second meeting, on Friday 16 August, saw the visit of the great American, Sprouts Elder, to the speedway now describing itself as 'the finest track in the country.' Despite the bad weather, some 3,000 saw the lanky Californian, regarded as the sport's unofficial world champion, wipe almost ten seconds off Carter's four-lap record (with a time of 89 seconds), win the Webb Challenge Trophy and dead-heat with Bristol's Len Parker in a match race. Parker won the Ty-Trist Handicap and the Flying Mile Scratch Race.

Team racing arrived on 30 August, when Monmouthshire faced Bristol. The home side was, in fact, drawn from well beyond the county borders and included Ron Whirlwind Baker, Ivor Hill, Nick Carter and Nobby Key. The visitors brought Billy Clibbett, Teddy Douglas, Ted Bravery and Stanley Gill. The four-heat contest ended 14-14, with heat wins for Baker, Carter, Bravery and Clibbett. In the individual competitions, George Gregor of Swansea won the Monmouthshire Handicap, ahead of Baker, though those positions were reversed in the Ferry, Hereford and Tredegar Trophy, while Baker beat Carter in the challenge races.

Speedway in Tredegar was being declared a huge success. After its first three meetings, it was said that the speedway had paid more in entertainment tax than the rugby club had taken in gross receipts for the whole previous season. The race meetings were bringing large crowds into the town and this was bound to have 'a beneficial influence', wrote one reporter.

The track was certainly attracting the big names, and on 6 September, Australian Vic Huxley was top of the bill. 'He is positively appearing, and dirt-track fans need not fear disappointment,' read the previous night's newspaper. But the following day it was a different story, with the headline 'Vic Huxley not present: A disappointment at Tredegar.' The speedway committee chairman, George Morgan, had the unenviable job of apologising to the expectant crowd, and explaining that a telephone call had confirmed Huxley and his manager had set off from London, but the meeting would have to go ahead without him. Extra match races were arranged, in which Len Parker beat Ron Baker, and Nick Carter beat Jack Luke, to set up a Parker-Carter final. However, it was a night of misfortune, and Parker was taken ill in the pits. Baker took his place, but was beaten by Carter. Parker won the Bedwellty Handicap Race and Baker the Webb Challenge Cup.

Australian Billy Lamont beat Jack 'Lightning' Luke in a series of match races on Monday 16 September, when he also won the Monmouthshire Flyers Scratch Race. Parker, however, took the honours in the Hereford and Tredegar Cup and the Cinder World Mile Handicap. Glyn Jones was taken to hospital after being thrown, but was found to have just a minor knee injury.

Team racing, of a sort, returned on Saturday 21 September with a contest for pairs. Bristol's Len Parker and Bill Clibbett won the match with 21 points, just one ahead of Cardiff's Jack Luke and Champ Upham. Salford pair Fred Williams – not to be confused with the future Welsh world champion of the same name (see Chapter Six) – and Arthur Wilcock were next with 13, and the Valleys pair of Baker and Carter last with 12. Lamont was back again, but had a miserable time: mechanical trouble saw him lose the match races against Len Parker 2-0 and fail to figure in the Town Clock Handicap. In the Lamont Scratch Race, Stan Longney fell in front of him, forcing the Australian to pull up. Nobby Key won the handicap final and Parker the scratch race.

Tredegar's first season came to an end a week later, with Parker beating Clibbett and Upham beating local man Jack Wade of Risca in match races. Pontypridd's Tom Lougher won the £5 first prize in the Bevan Handicap, and Parker achieved the same prize for winning the Webb Challenge Cup.

The track re-opened on 22 April 1930, with two Stamford Bridge men, Colin Ford and Les Blakeborough as the star attractions, though neither made much impression – Ford losing the match race series to Parker, who also won the Flying Nine. Fred Hampson beat Tom Lougher to take the Powell Scratch Race. However, the season lasted only a couple of months, and by June the sport had lost another Welsh venue.

Caerphilly

Speedway returned to the Valleys in 1931, when a new track opened in Caerphilly. Press reports described the Virginia Park Stadium as 'one of the finest sports grounds in the country' and certainly the track was one of the biggest at a third of a mile. Its size meant races were run over three laps instead of the usual four on the standard quarter-mile oval.

Several thousand people braved the elements to witness the first meeting on Easter Monday, 6 April, when Caerphilly's own David Morgan officially opened the track by riding the first lap – to a huge ovation from the crowd. Jack Luke set the track record at 86 seconds, but came to grief

THE STADIUM, CAERPHILLY

DIRT TRACK RACING

On WHIT-MONDAY

ONE **1′3** PRICE

All the South Wales Cracks Definitely
Appearing. First Race 3.15. Car Park.
TOTALISATOR.
Refreshments on the Ground.
COVERED STANDS FOR ALL.

Caerphilly's meetings were unusual in having a trackside 'tote' – an innovation which did not please the sport's authorities.

in the final of the Caerphilly Handicap, when his rear tyre burst and he was thrown. Although uninjured, the metal plate of his boot was torn clean off and he rode some distance with a bare foot.

Y. Davies finished ahead of Champ Upham in that final, while Upham took the honours in the Virginia Park Scratch Race. In match races, Pip Price beat Y. Davies, David Morgan beat Tom Lougher and John Wade beat Fred 'Hurricane' Hampson.

Surprisingly, there seem to have been no further meetings in 1931, but the sport came back the following year – with a new twist. While other Welsh tracks had tried to lure the fans with appearances by big-name riders, Caerphilly introduced trackside betting. No doubt inspired by the totalisator run for greyhound racing at the venue, organisers installed a 'tote' for the bikes. So, on Whit Monday, 20 May 1932, spectators were promised two and a half hours' entertainment in comfort – with vast covered accommodation and betting on some events. A 'record crowd' saw T. Crocker win both the Caerphilly Handicap and the Castle Handicap, but he missed out on a clean-sweep when he was thrown in the final of the Virginia Park Handicap, which went to Durrin John.

The meeting was judged to be so successful that the promoters announced they would run events fortnightly and that everything was being done to make Caerphilly the premier 'motor-tote' track in the country. Advertisements for the next meeting, on Saturday 4 June, were less modest: 'The finest and fastest track with the finest and fastest riders.' The track boasted a large car park, covered stands, first-class refreshment rooms and club bar, with Cardiff just half an hour away by train or bus.

One punter at this event apparently backed a surprise heat winner by mistake and won 74 shillings (£3.70) for his 2 shilling (10p) stake. To give an idea of the value of that win, admission prices for this meeting were 1 shilling and 2 pence (6p) or 2 shillings and 4 pence (12p).

After Roy Zeal had got the better of Eddie Hopkins to win the Keiswetter Handicap, the final of the Glamorgan Handicap became another duel between the two. The crowd was said to be on tiptoe as Hopkins forced his machine to the post to win by the narrowest of margins. John Wade went on to beat Hopkins in a match race.

Hopkins was on form again at the next meeting on Wednesday 15 June, finishing ahead of Tom Lougher to win the Pauline Gower Handicap, while the Crimson Circus Handicap went to H.J. Lea. The only accident of the night involved J. Evans of Newport, who suffered minor facial injuries in a fall.

Despite the promise of fortnightly meetings, a month went by before the season's fourth dirt-track races were finally arranged for Wednesday 13 July. As an experiment, races would now be over four laps, instead of three, making each race a mile and a third, and because of the 'prevailing financial conditions,' admission prices were reduced to 1 shilling and 3 pence for the centre stand and 7 pence for the side stands.

As it turned out, heavy rain forced the meeting to be postponed to the following Saturday, when the July Handicap and the County Handicap were the main events. Results from the meeting are not known, but the advertised line-up was less impressive than for some earlier events, with Luke, Upham and Hampson among the notable absentees.

This was to be the last speedway event at Virginia Park. The local press seemed to have lost interest to the point that the reasons for the track's closure appear to have gone unreported. However, those difficult financial conditions may well have contributed to its demise. It should also be noted that motorcycle racing's governing body, the ACU, prohibited betting at speedways, and earlier that same year, 1932, had withdrawn its licence from Lea Bridge in London for running a trackside 'tote'. Concerns were expressed at Lea Bridge that riders were being paid to lose races, and the tote was abandoned after a few weeks. Whatever the reasons, Caerphilly's closure marked the end of speedway in the Valleys for a further three decades.

Neath

Leslie Maidment, the man who had taken speedway back to Cardiff in 1951, looked further west the following year and applied to open a track at Neath Abbey. Construction work began, and Welsh speedway legend Freddie Williams – who had won the world championship in 1950 and would do so again in 1953 – planned to run a training school there. Williams, who had made his name at Wembley, and with the England team around the world, was born in Port Talbot, just a few miles from the proposed Neath track (see Chapter Six).

However, the post-war speedway boom was starting to decline, and without adequate finance, the track remained incomplete and unopened. It did see motor sport of the four-wheeled variety in 1955, when London-based businessman Derek Walker ran a season of stock car racing at the venue. The 375-yard track, incongruously overlooked by the abbey ruins, hosted twelve car meetings that year, attracting large crowds and top drivers from around Britain, but it lasted just that single season.

The venue lay disused for several years, until New Zealander Trevor Redmond came along in 1962 with the aim of running a team in the Provincial League. This competition had been launched in 1960, and revived speedway – albeit at a lower level than the National League – at several venues which had closed during the 1950s. Redmond was already known on the Welsh scene as the top man at Aldershot, who had been rivals of Cardiff a decade before (see Chapter One), and had won the Provincial Riders Championship in 1960. The energetic Kiwi threw himself into the project, with the intention of being promoter, manager and rider, and he had to overcome numerous hurdles, including less than ideal living conditions. He, his wife, Pat, and young daughter lived in a caravan on the site, while work on the track was underway. As launch day neared, South Wales suffered an outbreak of smallpox, and the public was advised not to go to places with large numbers of people. Redmond pressed on with plans for an opening challenge match against Wolverhampton Wolves on 21 April, but more bad luck was to follow – torrential rain forced the meeting to be called off.

So the Neath team, usually billed as the *Welsh* Dragons in an effort to win support from beyond the town, made its debut two days later on

Trevor Redmond, the driving force behind Neath Dragons.

The programme cover for the first Neath fixture – a challenge match at Cradley on 23 April 1962.

Three young members of the Dragons' team. From left to right: Freddy Powell, George Major and Jon Erskine. Powell and Erskine were both in their first speedway season.

Easter Monday, in a challenge match at Cradley Heath. Redmond won Neath's very first race, but the match ended in a 46-32 defeat. Dragons' team included local find Glyn Chandler, who made a great debut with two heat wins, and another youngster Jon Erskine, son of a famous speedway father, Mike. Erskine senior was an old Etonian who became a top-level rider with Wimbledon and was now the manufacturer of speedway bikes. Jon had just one year of grass-track experience under his belt when he made his speedway debut, and although he failed to score in this opening fixture, he went on to become a key member of the Neath team.

After the previous week's wash-out, Neath made their home debut on Saturday 28 April in a challenge match against Sheffield. Some 3,000 turned out to see Dragons win 41-37.

The early season Southern Cup proved a disappointment, however. Neath lost heavily in all three away fixtures – at Plymouth Devils (46-32), Exeter Falcons (51-26) and Poole Pirates (51-22). The only Dragons win in the competition was 41-37 at home to Plymouth. They lost the home match with Poole 47-31 and the Exeter visit was another victim of the South Wales weather – a downpour half an hour before the first race forced the match to be called off.

Poole's Australian Geoff Mudge and Dragons' George Major – on loan from Oxford – shared the honours in the Wales and West Trophy on 5 May, but when the league programme started Neath took time to find

NEATH ABBEY
Speedway

SATURDAY, 26th MAY, 1962

at 7 p.m.

WELSH
DRAGONS v. POOLE
PIRATES

PROGRAMME - - - - 6D.

The programme cover from Dragons' Southern Cup clash with Poole Pirates. Neath lost 47-31, and would eventually finish behind Poole in the Provincial League title chase.

Roy Taylor had missed all of 1961 through injury, but became a useful member of the Neath side.

their form. Redmond was ruled out for the first few meetings, after suffering a broken collarbone in the Cup match against Poole, but South African Howdy Cornell arrived in time for the first Provincial League match at home to Cradley Heath on 1 June. He scored an impressive 9, as did Erskine, but Roy Taylor, with 8, was the only other to score more than two points, and Neath lost 34-44. Taylor had returned to the sport after a year's absence following a late-season injury while riding for Bristol in 1960. The next day Neath travelled to Stoke and were only two points behind going into the final heat, but neither visiting rider finished and the 5-0 score gave Potters a 42-35 win.

There was a break in league action on 9 June when Neath hosted a world championship qualifying round. Middlesborough's Eric Boothroyd took the honours, with a 15 points maximum. Redmond, back from injury, was second – having dropped just one point when he finished second to the Bears rider in the fastest race of the night.

The Welsh fans had more to cheer the following week, when Dragons beat visiting Wolverhampton 47-31. While Redmond led the scoring with 10, the points were well distributed throughout the team, suggesting greater consistency. Off the track, a new 'drive-in' spectator facility was being announced and, with typical Redmond humour, there would be 'no extra charge for Rolls, Cadillacs or Bentleys'.

However, such initiatives did little to boost crowds, and in mid-summer the team moved more than 200 miles to St Austell in Cornwall, which had a captive audience of holidaymakers eager to be entertained. During its Cornish break, the team rode as 'St Austell Gulls incorporating Welsh Dragons', and notable successes included a 40-38 win at Cradley Heath – the first time in three years that the Heathens had lost at home – and a 51-27 destruction of Bradford Panthers at 'home' in Cornwall. It was said that the top teams were suffering 'chronic indigestion' from this mixture of Cornish pasty and Welsh rarebit, and the Neath/St Austell side were looking like challengers for the title.

Back at Neath on 4 August, against Poole, the bad luck which had plagued the promotion returned, when the track was flooded by rain, the team suffered a series of mechanical failures which led to defeat, and then there was a power cut. It meant elastic to start the races instead of the usual electric gate, red flags at the corners instead of lights, and no hot water in the riders' showers.

Down in St Austell later that month, a three-team contest saw Glyn Chandler, Charlie Monk, Jon Erskine and Howdy Cornell riding for Wales, while Redmond led Cornwall, and a Midlands team completed the line-up.

It was an eventful debut season by any standards, but poor crowds ensured Dragons' first would also be their last. The geography of the track presented another problem, enabling hundreds of spectators to

★★★★★★★★★★★★★★★★★★★★★★★

CORNISH STADIUM
ST. AUSTELL
Tuesday, 17th July, 1962

Lucky Programme

AT 7.45 P.M.

N⁰ 1072

St. Austell Gulls
(Incorporating Welsh Dragons) V.
Stoke Potters
Provincial League Champ.

SPONSORED BY SENIOR SERVICE CIGARETTES

Official Souvenir Programme 9d.

★★★★★★★★★★★★★★★★★★★★★★★

When the Dragons were Gulls: Neath's 'home' fixture against Stoke was one of several run 200 miles away in Cornwall. The small print shows the St Austell Gulls to be 'incorporating Welsh Dragons'.

watch the action from outside for free. The final meeting took place on 1 September, when Neath beat Sheffield 41-36, in a match postponed from 11 August, to end their only season as runners-up behind Poole in the Provincial League, having won 14 and drawn one of their 24 matches. The track was later demolished to make way for industrial development. Redmond, a true leader of his team, topped the club scoring with an average of 8.6.

Among the real triumphs of the eventful Neath experiment had been the discovery of Jon Erskine, who enjoyed a superb debut season, becoming a heat leader in a matter of weeks, and gave three superb performances in the Provincial Riders Championship, only to miss the final through injury. Towards the end of the season, the nineteen-year-old was involved in one of the sport's most spectacular accidents, when he was thrown over the safety fence at Leicester. Erskine was among those who would return to Wales – after spending 1963 with Long Eaton, he would become a founder member of Newport Wasps.

Neath Dragons – runners up in their only season. From left to right, back row: Brian Leamon (manager), George Major, Jon Erskine, Charlie Monk. Front row: Trevor Redmond, Roy Taylor, Howdy Cornell, Glyn Chandler.

3

NEWPORT

No town or city in the Principality has embraced the sport with more enthusiasm than Newport in south-east Wales. Somerton Park was a speedway venue for fourteen successive seasons in the 1960s and '70s, and after a twenty-year absence Newport again became home to the Wasps in 1997 with the opening of the purpose-built Hayley Stadium.

Somerton Park

Newport missed out on the early speedway boom in South Wales, but Somerton Park, the Newport County soccer ground, did hold a few grass-track meetings in the late 1920s and early '30s. One such event, organised by Newport and Gwent Motor Club on 14 June 1930, attracted riders from across the region. Newport's own Idris Jones set the fastest time of the day and won the 500cc competition. The 350cc event went to J. Christopher of Pontypool and the 250cc race to A. Harris of Newport.

It was more than three decades later that true speedway arrived in Newport when, two years after the brief appearance of Neath Dragons, Newport Wasps were launched. Wolverhampton rider Cyril Francis lived in Newport and suggested to Wolves boss Mike Parker that Somerton Park might be a suitable venue for a new track. Greyhound racing at the stadium had finished in 1963 and it looked a good site for the bikes to move in. Although hardly modern – it dated back to the soccer club's formation in 1912 – it boasted cover on three sides, seating for several hundred and even a viewing bar, which was unusual for British stadia in the 1960s.

Parker was a multi-track promoter with interests in speedway and stock car racing around Britain. He and co-promoter Charles Foot brought in Peter Vandenberg, Dick Bradley and Alby Golden from Southampton, whose track had been sold for redevelopment, as the basis of the new team. Jon Erskine, the big discovery of Neath's only season (see Chapter Two), also joined the line-up from Long Eaton and helped construct the track, a 376-yard circuit which had to be a near-oblong shape to accommodate the soccer pitch.

The great 'discovery' of 1964 was the talented Bob Hughes.

The team would be called the Wasps, after the amber and black colours also worn by the town's rugby and soccer teams. They entered the Provincial League and entertained Cradley Heath in their opening home fixture on Good Friday, 17 April 1964. An estimated 10,000 turned out to see their new team in a 38-40 defeat.

Such enthusiasm in numbers – the vital ingredient which Neath had lacked – was a hallmark of that debut season. One night, fans queued in pouring rain, which had officials on the verge of cancelling the meeting. But the crowd grew, they decided to go ahead – and more than 7,000 watched even in that terrible weather.

Bradley enjoyed a superb season, after a broken arm had curtailed his 1963 campaign. He finished top of the Wasps' scorers with a total of 339 points from his 37 matches for an average 9.1. Vandenberg was second with 312 from 32 (average 9.75) and Golden completed the ex-Southampton trio in third place with 311 points from 32 (average 9.7). Newport could hardly have had a better debut season – they won the Knock Out Cup and finished a highly satisfactory fourth in the twelve-team Provincial League. They also made a local discovery in Bob Hughes, a highly impressive debutant, who ended the season with 68 points from his 19 matches. Newport's presence also added an extra international dimension to events across the border. On 29 June 1964, for example, four Newport men – Bradley, Erskine, Golden and Vandenberg rode as Wales in a four-team tournament at Exeter. They finished third behind winners Scotland and runners-up England, but ahead of the Overseas quartet.

Newport's cup victory did not come easily. Indeed, the final against Cradley seemed jinxed from the start. One of the biggest crowds of the season gathered at Somerton Park for the first leg on 25 September, but the match was delayed by fifteen minutes because two of the visiting riders had not arrived. There was a further hold-up when the starting gate failed, and then the public address system broke down.

However, on the track things went better for Wasps. The home side took an early 4-point lead and, although Cradley had levelled the scores after six heats, Newport went on to win the first leg 58-38, with Bradley and Vandenberg scoring 13 each and Erskine adding 10.

The 20-point lead was a useful cushion to take to the Midlands almost a month later for the deciding leg on 24 October. For the first seven heats, it looked more than adequate for the Welsh side to secure the silverware. By this stage, Heathens had only managed to reduce the deficit by two. From that point, however, Cradley hit back hard and closed the gap steadily until it all rested on the very last race. Newport needed 2 points (a second place) to secure the cup. Cradley's John Hart won the race, but Bradley took a comfortable second to give Newport a thrilling 97-95 aggregate win.

As 1965 arrived, so did a new league structure: the Provincial League was gone and a new single-tier British League would involve all 18 teams. This would be a much tougher competition, but Wasps added just one name to their squad – Australian veteran Jackie Biggs. He had been close to winning the World championship in 1951, before finishing third, but his best days seemed to be behind him. At Coventry in 1964 he had averaged just 3.5 points per meeting, but his career revived as soon as he arrived in Wales. Newport's first match was away to mighty Wimbledon. They lost by just two points and Biggs scored a maximum. Some observers said it was a fluke, but Biggs's rediscovered form continued with a top-scoring nine in the next match at Exeter, and a total of 32 paid points from his next three. It was no fluke – he ended the season as Wasps' top scorer with an average of nine.

Erskine suffered a hand injury early in the year, but came back strongly, and Bob Hughes continued the progress he had shown in his first year. Indeed, his form at reserve was so convincing that Newport allowed Vic White to switch to Belle Vue – a move cheekily described by Wasps as 'helping out the former big boys'. Their home form was superb – they won every league match at Somerton Park, and a clutch of home matches early in the fixture list saw them among the pace-setters in the table, but away form let them down badly. They won only two matches of their 17 on the road, both against injury-weakened opponents at Cradley Heath and Long Eaton, and their away results included a record 64-14 defeat at Wolverhampton. Bradley broke his arm in July, when he had been averaging 7.99 points, and he missed the rest of the season. Wasps were unable to find a suitable replacement, although White returned for a while, and their form suffered accordingly. The cup was lost at the first hurdle when Newport had the misfortune to be drawn away to mighty West Ham in the second round, after receiving a bye in the first. Predictably, the Welsh side lost 56-40.

However, it was a more than satisfactory second season, with a sixth place finish in a much stronger league, and attendance continued to be the envy of many more established clubs. When Newport hosted a test match between Great Britain and the Soviet Union, there were an estimated 19,000 crammed into Somerton Park, with extra seating installed over the pits area.

In 1966, Swedish star Gote Nordin arrived, and almost single-handedly saved the club from humiliation. Biggs's form had been impressive the previous year – indeed it was one of the speedway talking points of 1965 – Nordin's form this season was little short of sensational. He scored 80 more points in two fewer matches – with an average of 10.40, and he won the individual Internationale at Wimbledon, one of the sport's most prestigious titles.

There were other changes in the line-up, with Vandenberg leaving for Wolverhampton, Bradley failing to return after his injury the previous season, and Vic White heading for Long Eaton. Golden announced he was retiring, but new manager Ken Sharples persuaded him to stay – though his form was disappointing and he ended the year with an average of just 5.34.

This was the year when Nordin's form was almost all that mattered. The team was almost totally reliant on him collecting a big total in every match. On the occasions when he didn't – such as the home defeat by Newcastle in May when he was thrown over the fence and scored just two all night – the team suffered. Wasps' proud unbeaten home record had been lost to Exeter Falcons earlier in the month, and this night was even more miserable. At one point, Sharples had approached Newcastle Diamonds star – and future world champion – Ivan Mauger to loan a bike to a Newport rider, only to be refused.

Before the month had ended, there was more trouble at home, when the match against Wolverhampton on 30 May was called off because of a strike by members of the riders' union, the Speedway Riders Association, over the use of guests.

Biggs had a troubled year, with injuries and a disagreement with management which saw him quit for two weeks. He ended the season with 170 points from 23 matches (average 7.23), compared with 306 points from 34 matches in 1965. Erskine improved and finished with an average of 6.03, but others had averages of below 5.5, and although Tim Bungay looked a promising acquisition in June, his season ended when he broke both legs.

With a zero success rate away from home and inconsistent form at Somerton Park, Newport finished a disappointing seventeenth in the league and again exited the Knock Out Cup in their first match, this time 36-60 at Belle Vue, after another first round bye. Nordin's star status was enhanced when he reached the world championship final, through the Swedish rounds, while Erskine got as far as the semi-finals.

Nordin left for Poole, and was replaced by his compatriot, Torbjorn Harrysson. While Nordin had been a clinical, efficient rider, Harrysson was a spectacular, forceful racer. One observer remarked that Gote had the crowd applauding, while 'Toby' had them screaming. Oxford's Jimmy Gooch replaced Biggs, who had gone to Cradley, and John Bishop, also from Oxford, filled the place of Geoff Penniket.

Wasps were hit by early season injuries to Jon Erskine and Cyril Francis – both suffering concussion in separate incidents. Then Bob Hughes broke his wrist. Rumours that Francis was seeking a return to Wolves proved unfounded, and when Erskine returned he was in brilliant form, becoming the first British rider to score an 18-point maximum away from home – and that at high-flying Poole. But another injury put him back on the sidelines, and Hughes seemed to return too soon and never got back to the form of which he was known to be capable.

Further down the order, there was the mystery of Alan Paynter, who failed to score a single point in his 12 rides over seven matches for Newport, but when loaned to Belle Vue for a challenge match he was their top scorer. More significantly, Harrysson missed too many matches because of commitments back home, and Wasps struggled without him. They lost their last five matches, including one at home, and suffered two crushing 60-18 defeats at West Ham and Halifax, in the space of four days. On all three occasions, Harrysson was absent.

They held first place in the table for a while, but in the end did well to finish twelfth. Harrysson had the best average with 10.05, but missed nine matches, so Gooch's 335 was the highest points total. Sharples resigned before the end of the campaign and was later killed in a car crash. In a horrible coincidence, his successor Eddie Glennon would suffer a similar fate the following year.

For 1968, expansion meant the league was split into two divisions, with Wasps in the nineteen-team top flight. Harrysson was again the star of the show, but he missed even more matches this year, and though he averaged 9.73, both Gooch and Erskine contributed more points. Harrysson missed fifteen matches in all, either because of demands from Sweden or injury. He suffered a suspected broken foot in an incident at

The programme cover from Newport's 1968 league match with Swindon Robins. Despite a score of 13 by ex-world champion Barry Briggs, the visitors were soundly beaten 47-31.

the Wimbledon Internationale on 3 June. X-rays revealed no break, but the Swede earned manager Glennon's praise for riding despite considerable pain in the home win over Coatbridge (Edinburgh) Monarchs on the following Friday and the defeat at Coventry next night. 'Harry' was also a key member of the Swedish national team competing in the World league that year, and reached the individual world final, ending the night with 10 points.

At home, Newport won 17 of their 18 matches, but they failed to register a single point on opponents' territory, and ended the season a lowly thirteenth. Again, there was an early exit from the Knock Out Cup. Drawn away to Poole, after a bye in round one, Wasps lost 52-56 on 22 April. Long-serving captain Alby Golden finished with a disappointing average of 5.72, while local men Erskine and Francis were both hampered by injuries – though Francis won Newport's world championship qualifying round on 31 May.

Norman Strachan started the season well, before being sidelined through injury, only to return in stunning form, showing he could step in to a heat leader's slot when required and returning double-figure scores with regularity. Jimmy Gooch enjoyed a consistently good season and ended the year as Wasps' second highest scorer with an average of 7.97, while Bob Hughes was reckoned to be the team's most improved performer. Between 20 September and 4 October, he recorded three

The Wasps of 1968. From left to right: Jon Erskine, Bob Hughes, Torbjorn Harrysson, Cyril Francis, Norman Strachan, Alby Golden, Jimmy Gooch.

Newport's 1969 line-up. From left to right, standing: Chris Julian, Einar Egedius, Cyril Francis, Jon Erskine, Bob Radford (manager), Sandor Levai; (on machine) Alby Golden. Kneeling: Norman Strachan, Terry Shearer.

successive scores of 12 in home wins over Glasgow, Newcastle and Exeter, followed by a paid 15 at Cradley and 10 at Hackney. Terry Shearer, in his debut season, moved in and out of the side as injuries opened gaps. In his 64 rides in 28 matches, he scored 28 points and 5 bonuses, suggesting greater contributions to come. Another debutant was smiling Dai Evans, a regular with Division Two Crayford Highwaymen, who showed promise in his 3 matches for Wasps.

Crowds remained encouraging, largely due to the efforts of Glennon, and anticipation of another Test match between England and the Soviet Union on 5 July prompted the rare measure of selling advance tickets for the grandstand. England won, incidentally, 68-40, with Martin Ashby totalling 17 points, and setting a new track record of 66.6 seconds. Glennon's death in a road accident later that month cast a gloom over Somerton Park for the rest of the season.

A row between Swedish riders and the British Speedway Promoters Association meant Newport, now under the managership of Bob Radford, lost the services of Harrysson for 1969. He did ride in the World Final at Wembley, however, but broke his leg so badly that he was out of action for three years. Into Harrysson's place, former Hungarian refugee Sandor Levai arrived reluctantly from Belle Vue. He had tried for years to break through, but couldn't afford competitive machinery. However, in his late thirties he would top the Newport scorecharts for three seasons as the team continued to struggle.

Wasps were also without Gooch, following a close-season transfer, and Francis was moved temporarily – and apparently reluctantly, under 'rider control' – back to Wolverhampton. Newport started superbly with a 51-26 home win over Newcastle on 4 April, but in only their third home league match, against Leicester Lions on 18 April, they dropped a point to record a 39-39 draw. Worse still, Bob Hughes and Norwegian newcomer Einar Egedius both suffered injuries, which would keep them out of action for several weeks, but Newport bounced back the following week with a 51-27 win over Oxford Cheetahs. Norman Strachan started the season strongly, but a bad fall aggravated an old shoulder injury and he rode much of the year against medical advice and often in severe pain, while Golden retired after 12 inconsistent meetings, which included a maximum sandwiched by two zeros. Erskine took over the captaincy, and introduced a successful junior training programme, but his own scoring suffered.

Newport again stayed only briefly in the Knock Out Cup, losing their first round match 54-24 at Leicester on 6 May. In the 19-team Division One, they finished seventeenth, again without any success away from home. Levai, of course, topped the scoring, with 365 from 37 matches for an average of 8.34. On three occasions, he scored as many or more points than the rest of the Wasps combined. Norman Strachan (6.29) and Chris Julian (6.06), who arrived from Cradley, provided the best support, but the latter broke his arm in an open meeting at Exeter at the end of the season.

Glennon was commemorated with the Eddie Glennon Memorial Trophy meeting on 1 August, won by New Zealand's former world champion Barry Briggs, who also took victory in the Prince of Wales Investiture Trophy on 27 June. Home honour was retained, however, with Levai's win in the world championship qualifying round on 23 May.

Levai stayed for 1970, but it was clear he needed some quality support, and diminutive New Zealander Bill Andrew was signed up for the job. Further international flavour was added with the arrival of Edgar Stangeland from Norway. The Norwegian started slowly, but the club persevered with him – resisting temptations to replace him with a better-known Swede, and by the end of the season he was returning some impressive scores. His end-of-season average of 6.38 was nothing startling, but was dragged down by his disappointing start. The figure placed him behind Levai (8.45) and Andrew (7.79) in the final averages, with none of the other regulars managing even to get near a five-points average. Bengt Brannefors' arrival from Sweden in mid-season was seen as a possible solution, but he did not live up to expectations, and left after 12 matches.

Swedish duo, Bengt Brannefors (left) and Tommy Johansson, were part of a cosmopolitan Wasps squad in 1971.

Individually, there were some successes. Andrew won the Newport world championship round on 1 May, and reached the semi-final where he scored eight points. Levai finished third in the Welsh Open Championship, won by Nigel Boocock, on 29 May.

However, the team finished at the foot of the league. Although they had managed to win two away matches during the season, they lost eight at home. The Knock Out Cup was another non-event for Wasps. Again they were beaten by Leicester, this time at home, 35-43 in the first round. Erskine suffered another early-season injury, this time a broken

Ronnie Genz (left) and Bill Andrew receive the admiration of female fans – and a trophy.

ankle, and moved to Wolves before the end of the year. Francis retired during the season, and Bob Hughes and Norman Strachan were both inconsistent.

The brightest spark was John Louis, a relative newcomer to the sport, loaned from Ipswich. He rode six matches for Newport and averaged eight points, including a maximum 15 at Wolverhampton. Wasps would have loved to have kept him, for he was clearly a star in the making – he went on to become British champion and England captain.

Newport boasted a really cosmopolitan squad for 1971. As well as Levai, Andrew and Stangeland, there was Sweden's Bengt Brannefors back again, this time with compatriot Tommy Johansson, Australian Dave O'Connor, Welshman Bob Hughes and Englishman Ronnie Genz. To add to the mixture, later in the season came Latvian Ted Laessing.

It was a successful mix, for Wasps ended the year in eighth place, and had enjoyed a 100 per cent home record, until their final match of the year on 1 October, when they lost to Hackney. Levai was top man again, his average of 8.76 putting him ahead of Johansson (8.03), Stangeland (7.87) and Andrew (7.24). The Knock Out Cup was the usual story – after a first round bye, they lost 32-46 at Kings Lynn. Levai also won Somerton

Sandor Levai remained Newport's top rider for three seasons, but his individual success was not matched by that of the team.

Newport's leading regular rider of 1972, Tony Clarke goes inside Poole's Crister Lofqvist, with Graham Plant close behind.

Park's rain-postponed world championship round on 30 April and the Southern championship round on 11 June.

However, the progress shown in 1971 was to be undone the next year. The trouble started in the winter, when virtually all the top men – Levai, Johansson, Stangeland, Andrew and Hughes – left. Genz and Laessing were retained, and in came Tony Clarke from Wembley, Graham Plant from Leicester, veteran Neil Street, and rising star Barry Duke. By any measure, the arrivals did not match the departures, and it seemed certain that Wasps, on their extended track, now measuring 413 yards, would be a weaker team.

Genz topped the averages, with just 7.45, but this was from just 14 matches in a season frequently and frustratingly interrupted by injury. Among the regulars, Clarke was the top man with a figure of 7.15 – a similar average to that which he had achieved with Wembley the year before. The difference was that with the Lions that score had placed him only fifth. Mid-season signings, Swede Bo Wirebrand and Phil Woodcock from Exeter, failed to lift the gloom, and Newport again finished the year with nothing to show from their away matches and with a miserable home record of 9 wins from 17. They achieved another unenviable record too – the 24-54 defeat by Kings Lynn was the biggest home loss in Division One history.

Newport's major individual events were won by visitors – Bruce Cribb taking the world championship round on 2 June and Denmark's world champion Ole Olsen the Prince of Wales Trophy on 9 August. There was one positive outcome – Wasps' first win in the Knock Out Cup since the British League was formed in 1965. After a first round bye, Newport beat Coventry 42-36 at home, before a decisive 20-58 third round defeat at Belle Vue on 5 August.

However, 1973 was to be a significant turning point in the Newport story, with the arrival of much-travelled Norwegian Reidar Eide. A major clear-out saw all but Street and Plant go, and both of them improved on their previous season's averages. Eide, like Nordin, Harrysson and Levai before him, was the team's undisputed number one, with a total of 325 points and an average of 9.77, but he had useful support from Plant (7.39), Roy Trigg (7.37) and Street (7.28). One of Plant's season highlights was his 13 points in a tight 38-40 defeat at Coventry on 18 August, when he also equalled John Louis' track record. Along with Eide and Trigg, he was also one of three Wasps to hold the Golden Helmet match race title during the season.

American Rick Woods proved a disappointing acquisition, however, quitting after a row over world championship eligibility. He was replaced by veteran Geoff Mudge, who was lured out of retirement and hit top form towards the end of the season, finishing with an average of 4.79. Peter Ingram, from Exeter, was a valuable addition too – he was

American Rick Woods had a disappointing spell at Newport in 1973. He is pictured in good form against Poole Pirates.

one of five Wasps to total more than 200 points, and finished with an average of 6.01.

The trouble was the vast majority of these points were still being scored at home, where Newport were beaten only once all year – and that by champions-to-be Reading Racers on a night when the Welsh side was without Eide. In away matches, for the fifth time in nine years, Wasps failed to bring back a point, and they finished the season tenth out of 18 teams in Division One. Away form had always been a Newport problem: end of season statistics produced by *Speedway Star* showed that in nine years of away matches, Wasps had won just nine and lost 150. This year, they came close on several occasions, however: 38-40 at Halifax on 7 April, at Wolverhampton on 20 April and at Coventry on 18 August, and an oh-so-close 38-39 at Kings Lynn on 29 September.

From 1974, the club ditched the 'Wasps' tag and operated without a nickname – the only team in the British League to do so. Australian Phil Crump arrived and, with Eide retained, Newport at last had two outstanding riders in their line-up. Plant and Ingram left in the close-season, but with Crump and Exeter's Bob Coles arriving, they looked set to build on their progress of the previous year. And so they did, thanks to an improvement in away form which saw two wins and three draws from their 16 road matches, while at home they again lost just one of the 16.

Crump was the star of the season, with a total of 421 points and an average of 10.79. He also won the *Speedway Star* Golden Helmet and broke the track record at Somerton Park, which had again been reconfigured to become a 390-yard course. His time of 66.2 seconds was set in a 40-38 win over Halifax Dukes on 28 June, during a hectic and eventful few days for the club. Just twenty-four hours earlier, they were crushed 27-51 at Wimbledon, after Eide had broken down en route to London, and twenty-four hours later, on 29 June, they found themselves 10 points behind at Swindon, before clawing back to record a 39-39 tie. Eide performed almost as well as he had the previous year, with an average of 9.42, and a place in the Anglo-American-Nordic final of the world championship. Street provided sound support with 7.70, as Newport finished sixth in the league. In the Knock Out Cup, they beat Swindon on aggregate in the first round, but lost both legs of the second round tie with Sheffield Tigers, bowing out with a 32-46 defeat at home on 5 July.

The following year, Crump, Eide and Street were joined by another Aussie star – teenager Phil Herne. Street and Crump were now using revolutionary new four-valve engines, converted Jawas known as 'Street specials'. These were the envy of riders throughout the league, just as Newport were becoming the envy of other teams. With four men

Close racing against Cradley United, with Roy Trigg leading the Newport challenge, as Jim Tebby goes wide.

The programme cover for the Knock-Out Cup second round decider in 1974, which Newport lost 32-46.

performing so well, the Welsh were – as manager Maurice Morley predicted – real challengers for the title. Crump was head and shoulders above the rest, ending the season with an average of 11.15, while the other three spent much of the year averaging around eight points, and battling for the heat leaders' positions. Eide finished on 8.99 and Herne on 8.70. Had it not been for a mid-season injury, which the veteran Street took a while to get over, Newport would have achieved the rare distinction of four riders averaging over eight. As it was, Street returned a figure of 7.32, as the team raced away to a third place finish, thanks to a 100% home record and vastly improved away form which saw 7 wins and a draw from their 17 matches. They led the table for a while, but were overtaken in the end by a superb surge from Ipswich and a clinically efficient team performance from Belle Vue.

Outside the top four riders, Newport also had Steve Gresham, an American who had walked out on Hull the previous year. His aggressive and spectacular style earned the praise of fans and the criticism of some rivals. Other riders making valuable contributions were Tom Owen, who divided his season between Newport and Newcastle, Bryan Woodward, recalled from Weymouth, and Bob Coles, who also helped get Mildenhall off the ground in the New National League (as Division Two had been renamed). At reserve, veteran Jim Tebby had a difficult season, made worse when he suffered mid-season injuries to his foot and knee, and promising youngster Mike Powell suffered a major setback when he was put in hospital after a late-season crash.

In the new Inter-League Knock Out Cup, Newport trounced New National League opponents Crewe Kings 58-20 in the first round on 28 April, before a crushing 28-50 defeat at Belle Vue in round two. In the *Speedway Star* Cup, for the top flight Gulf British League teams, they won both legs against Reading before facing Cradley in the second round. A convincing 49-29 win in the home leg seemed to have the match won, but United snatched an aggregate victory with a 51-27 win on their own track.

Crump reached the world final, where he bagged 10 points, and there were other Newport successes in the competition, with Eide reaching the European final and Gresham the Inter-Continental final, each scoring 3 points. Owen got to the semi-final and scored 4 points.

It was hard to see how things could get better for Newport – and they didn't. The 'rider control' system, to encourage equity among teams, forced Eide to leave for Leicester before the 1976 season, and the campaign started with three defeats. The season began at Hackney on 19 March, when new signing Neil Cameron failed to score, and Street managed only 2 points. While Gresham, Woodward, Herne and Crump performed well, Newport lost 42-36. It was three weeks before their next league match, at Halifax on 10 April. By then, Cameron had been

Reidar Eide gave fans and team-mates many reasons to celebrate during his three seasons at Newport, but moved to Leicester for the 1976 campaign.

replaced by Denmark's Preben Rosenkilde, and with no Street or Gresham, the Welsh side lost 38-40. A week later, at Belle Vue, they suffered a 23-55 hammering, and it became clear this would be a tougher season. Away defeats were perhaps no reason for despair, but 1976 would be a year of struggle.

Street retired in August after finding the going tougher than ever, particularly as he was also occupied with his four-valve engine conversions. American Gresham improved as the year went on, and finished with the club's second highest points tally (291) and third highest average (7.41). Crump was dominant again, with 488 points and an average of 10.57. He again reached the world final, and finished a sensational third. Herne showed good form too, but a serious back injury followed by a broken rib kept him out for a third of the season, and although his average was 9.70, that came from only 245 points. Another new name, Tormod Langli, was going well until his season ended with a broken wrist, and Rosenkilde's year was also curtailed through injury. Bob Coles was pulled back from Weymouth for 25 matches, Barney Kennett came on loan from Canterbury. Poland's Kaz Adamszak showed good form when he arrived from Exeter and another Australian Danny Kennedy looked a good prospect until he too succumbed to injury.

The all-important away form let Newport down again, with just a win and a draw from 18 matches, and it all added up to eighth place out of 18. Internationally, there was more cause for celebration, when Crump led the scoring as Australia won the World Team Cup for the first time, and Newport scored a humiliating 60-17 victory over the touring Poland team on 16 April.

So ended 1976, and for many that was the end – for the time being at least – of the Newport speedway story. Co-promoters John Richards and Pat Tapson had long wanted to take the sport back to Bristol, just across the Severn Bridge, and now they had a chance to do so at Bristol Rovers' soccer ground, Eastville. Around the same time, Newport County were doing well and had qualified for Europe by winning the Welsh Cup. They no longer needed or wanted speedway at Somerton Park and they increased the rent considerably.

Top Newport men Crump, Herne, Gresham, Coles and Woodward all became Bristol Bulldogs and raced on Fridays (Newport's traditional race night) at Eastville. Newport became the Dragons, dropped into the National League and ran on Wednesdays, but many fans simply stayed away. Coincidentally, the railway bend had been reshaped, extending the track to 416 yards, and many reckoned the new configuration provided some of the best speedway seen at Somerton park for many years. But manager Morley had an uphill struggle to enthuse the fans when Newport's former stars were racing in a higher league just over the border for the same promotion.

They switched back to Friday, now Bristol's race night, but the crowds stayed low. Woodward quickly returned and became Dragons' top scorer, with 322 points from 35 matches for an average of 8.31. Jim Brett led the averages with 8.84 from his 232 points in 25 appearances, having been appointed captain, despite having little league racing experience. John Goodall arrived from Sunderland and ended with an average 7.61, while Mike Broadbank, Cliff Anderson, Dave Shepherd and Malcolm Bedkober – son of former Exeter Falcon, Jack – contributed to a satisfactory campaign for the new team. Away form was again a problem, as it had often been for Newport sides. Dragons lost all 18 matches on the road, while at Somerton Park they won 16 and drew 2, to give them a twelfth place finish in the nineteen-team competition.

The 1977 season, and the era of speedway at Somerton Park, ended on 7 October, with the Dragons losing 36-42 to new league champions Eastbourne Eagles. The promotion declared they wanted to carry on, even though they had lost money in the lower league, but the decision was taken out of their hands. The soccer club refused to give the option of another season, and later lost its place in the Football League, finally going out of existence in 1993.

Before then, former Oxford, Long Eaton and Exeter speedway manager Roger Jones looked at reviving speedway at Somerton Park in the mid-1980s, but nothing came of his investigations, and there were further failed attempts in the early 1990s before the stadium was bulldozed to make way for housing.

Hayley Stadium

Speedway returned to Newport in 1997, on a purpose-built track run by a man devoted to the sport and the town. Tim Stone first saw the sport at Somerton Park as a young boy in the 1960s. 'I knew it was motorbike racing, but I didn't know what to expect,' he recalled. 'I thought it must be something to do with mods and rockers. When I saw the riders in their yellow and black jumpers, and people told me they rode for Newport, I couldn't at first understand what that meant.' But that soon changed. The smell of Castrol R and methanol, the noise and the colour made young Stone want to come back again and again. Years later, as well as being a mechanic for some of the riders, he even rode for a while, but had some bad falls. 'I couldn't do it,' he admitted. 'But it gave me an understanding of what the riders did and made me appreciate the skill they have.'

After launching and running a successful bookbinding business, Stone started looking at how he might bring speedway back to his home town. When Somerton Park was to be pulled down, he tendered successfully for all its equipment, including some 1,200 seats, floodlights and turn-stiles, and stored it at his house while he searched for a suitable location to revive the sport.

In 1996, the Welsh Development Agency handed over a 7.3-acre site on a 125-year lease, in the shadow of Llanwern steel works. A five-year search was over, but the work was only just beginning. There was less than six months to turn overgrown, sodden wasteland into a speedway stadium for the 1997 season. As well as the construction work, there was

Australian connection – star of today Craig Watson hears some words of advice from a veteran of the earlier Wasps era, Neil Street.

Anders Henriksson, one of the relaunched Wasps' first star signings, became a vital part of the Newport line-up for five years.

Paul Fry battles to retain control, as he is clipped by Newcastle's Nicky Pedersen in this 1998 encounter at Queensway Meadows.

the construction of the team to be done. A former Newport hero of the Somerton era, Neil Street, advised on the size and shape of the track, which measured 285 metres, and on the make-up of the new Wasps, who would compete in the Premier League – a second-level competition beneath the new Elite League. Reading's Phil Morris had been expected to be named as the team's star signing, but a deal could not be struck and instead Stone acquired Paul Fry from Exeter Falcons. An international flavour was added with the arrival of twenty-one-year-old Swede Anders Henriksson and young Australian Craig Watson. He signed Scott Pegler from Swindon and added two more on loan – Roger Lobb from Exeter and Martin Willis from Poole.

A promising, if somewhat inexperienced, team was in place. Now attention turned back to the stadium, where building control officers were insisting the two-metre exclusion rail, to keep supporters safely from the track fence, would need more posts and each would have to be sunk in a cubic metre of concrete. For five days, lorries brought in concrete from 5.30 a.m. to 10 p.m., in a process that added an unexpected £25,000 to Stone's bill. With everything in place, the riders finally got to test the track the day before the opening match against Exeter on 4 May. As the meeting got under way, unexpected heavy showers arrived, forcing the match to be abandoned with Wasps leading 22-8.

The next day there was worse news, when Fry suffered a serious back injury in a grass-track accident. It seemed likely that the man enlisted to lead the team in its debut season could miss the whole campaign, but luckily he was to return sooner than expected. However, Wasps had to start without him, and their opening match, at Arena-Essex on 9 May 1997 ended in a 38-51 defeat, although there were signs for optimism, not least the superb performance by Henriksson. Newport made their home debut on 18 May, when the unfancied Berwick Bandits snatched a 50-39 win in a meeting that saw Watson take a nasty fall. However, a first win was not far off – Henriksson again led the way, with firm support from Watson, in a 49-41 win over visiting Sheffield Tigers a week later.

A Friday and Saturday double-header in Scotland and the Borders on 6 and 7 June saw the return of Fry, though well below race fitness. Newport lost at Edinburgh and Berwick. In Friday's match in the Scottish capital, Martin Willis fell while leading heat three and suffered hand and shoulder injuries, and the next night on a soaking wet Berwick track, Henriksson went over his handlebars in his last heat and had to be kept overnight in hospital, while the rest of the team headed south for Sunday's home fixture against Oxford. Fry was now looking stronger, and he led his men to a 50-40 win over the Cheetahs. The next home match, against Exeter Falcons on 22 June saw the same scoreline, with Henriksson, Watson and Fry all in good form.

However, two wins in a row was as good as it got for Newport in this debut season. In the following six matches, there was one draw and five defeats – including a 29-61 reverse at Exeter, Wasps' heaviest loss of the season. Indeed, from their remaining 19 fixtures, Wasps recorded just four wins, on their way to the wooden spoon. Injuries played a part in the disappointing season – Henriksson broke his collarbone twice, Watson broke his leg and Scott Pegler broke his foot. However, Stone was not too upset at finishing at the foot of the league. For him, bringing the sport back to his home town was a success in itself. 'I'm not happy to be bottom,' he said at the end of the season. 'But after twenty years with no speedway I am not going to lose sleep – as long as we improve next year.'

As if building a new stadium during a wet winter and launching a new team in the tougher-than-expected Premier League was not enough of a challenge, Newport also ran a second team in the newly-named Amateur League. The Welsh Warriors emerged from Exeter's reserve team, the Devon Demons, and was run jointly with the Exeter management. The team rode half its home fixtures at Newport and half at Exeter – where the team was known as the Western Warriors. Roger Lobb, a member of the Wasps squad, was eligible to ride for Warriors while his Premier League average remained below four points, and his presence ensured good support for the venture at Queensway Meadows. His cousin, Gary

Lobb – a well-known name on the Cornish grasstrack scene – was also in the Warriors line-up. Roger led the end-of-season averages with 10.27, but he rode in only 10 matches because his Wasps score frequently ruled him out. Other promising names during the season, which saw them finish eighth of thirteen teams, included Paul Oughton, Richard Ford, Kevin Phillips, Paul Fudge, Andy Carfield – who rode in all 24 fixtures – and Chris Courage.

Roger Lobb was recalled by Exeter Falcons for the 1998 Premier League, leaving Stone to recruit two riders for an expanded seven-man team. In came Jon Armstrong and David Mason to join five retained from the opening season – Fry, Henriksson, Watson, Pegler and Willis. The stadium was improved with the opening of the grandstand, with its seats rescued from Somerton Park, and on paper, Wasps looked an improved side, but on the track they were disappointing. A miserable Premier League Cup campaign saw Wasps finish last of the six Southern group teams, and from their opening eleven competitive fixtures they had just one win and ten defeats.

Stone was determined to avoid another wooden spoon, and mid-season personnel changes saw Laurence Hare – who had been dropped by Oxford – and later sixteen-year-old prospect Chris Neath brought in to replace the injured Armstrong and the released Mason. Hare received a hero's welcome when he joined the line-up for the home clash with Edinburgh Monarchs on 5 July, but fell on the first bend of his opening heat. On the restart he went over again at almost the same point, and this time suffered a complex fracture at the lower end of his left leg. He had ridden less than 100 yards for his new club, and would miss the rest of the season, but his arrival marked something of a turning point for the club.

With Hare on his way to hospital, the team rallied round to score a 50-40 win over the Scots. The result sparked a seven-match winning streak, which ended on 14 August with the heaviest defeat of the season (29-61) at Edinburgh. Defeats at Berwick and Glasgow followed in successive days, before a dramatic home clash with Peterborough Panthers, who would go on to win the league. Four points adrift going into the final heat, Henriksson and Watson scored a 5-1 win to snatch a draw.

An eighth place finish in the league meant entry to the play-offs, and a tough first round match against table-toppers Peterborough. The English side won 48-40 at home, leaving Wasps with plenty of work in the return leg in Wales. In the end, Newport could not do enough, losing 47-42. An unpleasant incident saw Henriksson clash with Panthers' Nigel Sadler on the track, and several Wasps fans jump the fence to join in. Promoter Tim Stone warned that a repeat of such behaviour would lead to a lifetime ban, and he generously invited Sadler back to guest for Newport in two end-of-season challenge matches. After a shaky start, it had been a successful second term for the new club, one which was cemented by

Australian Frank Smart arrived from Exeter Falcons for the 1999 season and wowed the fans with his spectacular style.

Sixteen-year-old Andrew Appleton (to the right of the picture) earned his place with the Wasps, after proving himself with the Conference League Mavericks.

Bobby Eldridge takes a tumble in this 1999 encounter with Edinburgh Monarchs.

Anders Henriksson leads the way in a 1999 match against Reading Racers, with Scott Pegler (right) in close support.

Speedway as a contact sport? Tempers flare during the match with Glasgow Tigers on 6 June 1999.

the hugely popular Henriksson winning the Welsh Open Championship – only the second Newport rider to do so since the contest was inaugurated in the 1960s.

At amateur level there was reason for cheer as well. The two-home Warriors were replaced by Newport Mavericks, based firmly at Hayley Stadium and running in a new five-team Conference League. With the likes of Andrew Appleton, Chris Neath, Nick Simmons, Chris Courage, Richard Ford, Paul Oughton and Scott Pegler appearing in Mavericks colours, this was a strong young team. They won their first five matches on the trot and finished as runners-up behind St Austell Gulls.

As the Wasps prepared for 1999, Watson and Henriksson were retained, but Fry was released in favour of Australian Frank Smart from Exeter. Pegler stayed on as a key second-string man, and was joined by sixteen-year-old Appleton, who had proved himself in the Conference League, Chris Neath, retained on loan from Wolves, and Bobby Eldridge, who had shown promise at Reading and Long Eaton and had guested for Wasps the previous season.

Challenge match success over Reading Racers – with particularly pleasing performances from Neath, Appleton and Eldridge – was followed by the opening Premier National Trophy match at Exeter on 22 March. Smart crashed heavily, and was told his back injury would keep him sidelined for two months. Pegler took over as captain for a successful April, which saw a vital away win on the Isle of Wight put Wasps in contention to progress in the Trophy.

May brought more injury woe, when Anders Henriksson fell twice in the home trophy match with Reading on 2 May, the second time breaking his wrist. Newport won 57-32, but in that evening's return match up the M4, Reading got revenge with a 52-38 scoreline. Realising the plight the team now faced, Smart returned much earlier than planned, for the Premier League opener at home to the Islanders the next day. It was a brave move, and one which might have helped Wasps open the league campaign with a win had it not been for another bad fall, this time by Pegler, who also suffered a broken wrist as Newport went down 42-48.

Stone moved quickly to bring in Emil Lindqvist, who had impressed with the touring Young Sweden team, as a replacement for Henriksson, and made a useful debut in a 49-41 home win over Newcastle Diamonds on 9 May. He continued to perform well, prompting Stone to describe him as 'possibly the best team rider we have seen in a Wasps race-jacket in the modern era.' However, he suffered a dislocated shoulder in a controversial incident during a 47-46 home win over Glasgow Tigers on 6 June, when riders were involved in what might politely be described as a 'scuffle'. He returned a week later, but a heavy fall aggravated the injury and he opted for surgery, which ended his season.

In July, Newport won both legs of the Trophy semi-final over Swindon Robins, and their league form continued to impress. Of their eleven league matches from the beginning of August to the second week of September, they won ten, and in the 47-43 defeat at Arena-Essex on 27 August, they picked up a bonus point. They were helped by the return of Henriksson, but there was further disappointment, when they gave up a 16-point first-leg lead in the Knock Out Cup clash with Edinburgh to lose the tie on aggregate. With a challenge for league honours looking realistic and a Trophy final looming, Stone made another signing – bringing in Bjorn Gustafsson to replace the far-from-fit Pegler.

The first leg of the Premier National Trophy final at Edinburgh on 10 September saw the Monarchs take a 14-point lead, but Wasps recovered well to score a 48-44 win at Newcastle three days later, which secured second place in the league behind Sheffield Tigers. Sadly, that match saw Smart take another bad fall, which injured his shoulder sufficiently to keep him out of action for the rest of the year. For the deciding leg of the Trophy final, some 7,000 gallons of water had to be pumped off the Hayley Stadium track to allow the match to go ahead. After twelve heats, Edinburgh were still four ahead on aggregate. Henriksson and Watson produced a 5-1 win in heat thirteen to level the scores, and Appleton and Gustafsson did the same in the next race to put Wasps four ahead. A 4-2

Celebration – Craig Watson salutes the crowd as Newport clinch victory over Edinburgh in the 1999 Knock Out Cup decider ...

... and holds the cup aloft, as young fans congratulate their heroes.

last heat win made it a 93-87 aggregate victory for Newport, bringing the first trophy to Queensway Meadows.

Play-off wins over Berwick in round one and Exeter in the semi-final saw Newport in the Young Shield final against Sheffield. The clash followed the form book, with league winners beating league runners-up 98-82 on aggregate. There was more personal success for Watson, though – he followed Henriksson's example by winning the 1999 Welsh Open.

Wasps' success was mirrored by the Conference League's Mavericks, who – under the captaincy of Chris Neath – won the seven-team league with a formidable record which saw just two defeats in their twelve matches, making them the first Welsh team in speedway history to win a league title. Neath, along with Appleton and Eldridge had an exceptionally busy season, with commitments to the Premier League side as well as the Mavericks, meaning they rode as many as 82 meetings. Wins over Rye House Rockets, who had no home track and had to arrange fixtures at other venues, and Buxton Hitmen, took Mavericks to the Knock Out Cup final against St Austell Gulls. A first-leg lead of fourteen points had gone within the first five races of the deciding match in Cornwall, and Newport lost the tie by six points.

After the successes of 1999, anything less than a Premier League title would be a disappointment, and the Wasps finished 2000 a long way short of the title. Smart was not retained, Watson moved up to the Elite League, and Lindqvist proved too expensive to keep on. Henriksson, Neath and Appleton stayed, while Lee Herne was the first new name to be added. He was the nineteen-year-old son of Australian Phil Herne, who had ridden for Wasps in the 1970s. Also new for 2000 was Craig Taylor from Wolverhampton, Ben Howe, who had fallen out of favour with Ipswich in 1999, and former Wasp Jon Armstrong.

The defence of the Premier Trophy got off to a promising start, although the home win over Arena-Essex on 2 April was marred by a serious crash which left Howe with severe bruising to his back and Hammers' Nick Simmons with a broken leg. Home draws with Swindon and Isle of Wight later that month virtually ended any hopes of progress in the competition. Progress in the league was hampered by a series of injuries, eventually affecting every member of the team except Neath. Taylor needed three operations on his leg and Appleton broke his collarbone while guesting for Arena-Essex on 16 June – two days before his eighteenth birthday. Chris Courage – brought in from the Mavericks mid-season to replace Herne – suffered bruised ribs in the Knock Out Cup defeat at Workington on 10 June, Taylor had a back injury and Armstrong cracked vertebrae in a fall at Swindon on 20 July, which ended his season. Henriksson fractured his thumb and Howe's season ended with an arm fractured in 12 places – though not before he had broken the track

The Wasps of 2000. From left to right: Jon Armstrong, Ben Howe, Anders Henriksson, Chris Neath, Andrew Appleton, Lee Herne, Craig Taylor, Gavin Morrison (manager).

Rising star Chris Neath was the only Wasp to escape injury in the 2000 season. He is pictured alongside Anders Henriksson.

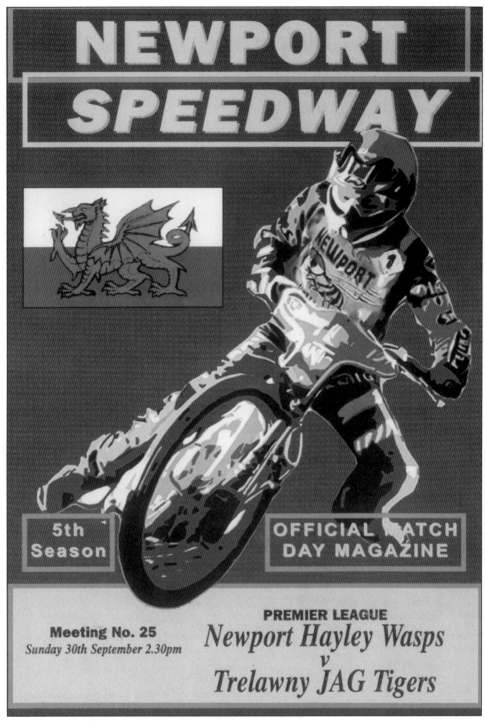

Programme cover for the end-of-season clash with Trelawny Tigers in 2001. The match looked set to decide the wooden spoon, but Newport were already condemned to the bottom place.

record with a time of 58.45 seconds in the 52-40 win over Newcastle on 16 July. Wasps finished a lowly tenth out of 14 clubs in the Premier League. Henriksson again topped the averages with 8.68, ahead of Howe on 8.27.

The Mavericks had an even harder act to follow after their championship-winning season and, like the senior team, they suffered a disappointing 2000. Pegler (9.97) and Courage (9.30) returned impressive averages, but the team finished fifth in the ten-team Conference League.

For 2001, the Wasps squad looked promising, but it was to be a year of even bigger disappointment. Former England international Glenn Cunningham was joined by the fiery Steve Masters and – in time for the league season – the dependable Anders Henriksson, as well as promising first-year Australian Scott Smith. Rising star Chris Neath was unavailable for the start of the season, after breaking an ankle in Australia over the winter. His place was taken by the returning Emil Lindqvist, until he recovered. Tommy Palmer and Nick Simmons filled the reserve slots initially, although Rob Finlow, Martin Williams, Carl Wilkinson and a string of guests all made appearances. Two home defeats in the Premier National Trophy, against Swindon (41-48) on 15 April and Reading (43-47) in the last Southern Section match on 20 May condemned Wasps to bottom place in the group. Then came the first round of the Knock Out Cup and a 26-64 destruction at Exeter, leaving Newport with a deficit which they could never hope to recover in the home leg. So just the league was left, but the campaign began with seven straight defeats, three of them at home, and it became clear Wasps were not going to be challenging for honours this year.

Another succession of injuries contributed to the failure, and forced Stone to enlist more than twenty guests during the season. Wasps never won away, and they lost seven home league matches. There was a brief period of hope in mid-season, when they hit some consistency at home, but it did not last. As the league wound down, Newport were again in danger of finishing at the foot of the table. It seemed that the final match at home to Trelawny would settle the wooden spoon, but by the time the fixture came around on 30 September, the Cornish team had done enough to condemn Newport, and Wasps' 64-26 win – their biggest ever in the Premier League – counted for nothing.

With the poor results had come poor crowds – a situation exacerbated by economic gloom in the town following 3,000 redundancies at the steel works next to the stadium. For the Mavericks, too, it was a poor season, with 5 wins from their 16 matches leaving them seventh in the eight-team league. Scott Pegler led the scoring with an average of 9.49, and inspired the side to some encouraging performances. Martin Williams, Rob Finlow, Graig Gough, Tom Brown and Ryan Tolley all showed signs of progress – and that has always been the aim of the Conference League side.

Not just solo – Newport hosted the 2001 British Open Championship for sidecars.

Aussie stars making a welcome return for 2002. Above: Frank Smart (seen in spectacular sideways style, centre of picture). Below: Craig Watson (celebrating another win with a wheelie).

Scott Pegler (right of picture) led the Mavericks into 2002. He is seen here in the opening heat of the all-Wales clash with Carmarthen, duelling with Dean Felton.

Promoter Tim Stone said success for Mavericks would be judged by bringing on young riders, not necessarily by winning silverware.

Developing young talent goes hand-in-hand with developing the stadium at Newport. A new-look Wasps team was put together for 2002. Back came Australians Craig Watson and Frank Smart, and another Aussie, Scott Smith, was retained. The seven was completed by a quartet of Englishmen – Ben Howe, Lee Dicken, Barrie Evans and Carl Wilkinson. After defeating Reading Racers in the two-leg pre-season M4 Challenge, their first competitive outing was the Premier Trophy opener against hotly-tipped Swindon Robins. Wasps, supported by returning sponsors Hayley Bearings, held an injury-hit Wiltshire side to a 48-42 win on their own track on 21 March, before crushing them 57-33 in Wales three days later to win 99-81 on aggregate. Watson led the way with a 15-point maximum, but there was bad news for Howe who suffered a serious fall, which required a trip to hospital for stitches.

The 2002 season also saw the Mavericks re-emerge after close-season uncertainty, thanks to new sponsorship from the GMB Union. The previous year's top scorer, Scott Pegler, led the side, which also included Simon Walker, Jamie Holmes, Rob Finlow, Carl Wilkinson, Danny Warwick and sixteen-year-old newcomer Karl Mason. Although they lost their opening match, an historic all-Wales clash with the new Carmarthen Dragons (see Chapter Five), there were encouraging signs in their first performance. In addition, Newport introduced a sidecar speedway team for a proposed national league, following the successful hosting of the 2001 British Championship. The spring of 2002 saw the town achieve city status, and Hayley Stadium, with its long lease, remained one of the few UK venues used exclusively for speedway. Although 'expert' predictions suggested Wasps would finish in the lower reaches of the Premier League, the long-term future was looking bright for Newport speedway.

4

THE LONG TRACKS

Long-track racing, a form of speedway on ovals of roughly a kilometre or half a mile, has always been more popular in mainland Europe than in Britain, but Wales has hosted the sport at two venues – Ammanford in the South West and Prestatyn in the North, both of them pony-trotting tracks.

Prestatyn

The North Wales holiday resort of Prestatyn gained a new tourist attraction in 1967, when Motherwell speedway owner George Kennedy constructed a half-mile track, with a crushed limestone, granite and coral surface. Long-track and grass-track specialist Don Godden took the honours in the opening meeting, which attracted many of the sport's top names.

A later meeting, promoted by the local Point of Ayr Motorcycle Club, on 30 August, involved another impressive line-up. Malcolm Simmons beat Ivan Mauger to the line in the first semi-final, while Howard Cole finished ahead of late entry Chris Pusey in the second. New Zealander Mauger, a future world champion, took the honours in the final, averaging 53.9mph and finishing ahead of W.G. Allan, who went on to lift the trophy in the second solo competition.

The programme also featured sidecars, with Paul Pinfold taking his 650cc Triumph to victory. Like Mauger, Pinfold would go on to greater things, establishing himself as one of the most influential figures in combination racing and setting up the ambitious World of Rebels sidecar series some twenty years later. In a second competition that day, however, Pinfold could only finish third, with honours going to Lawson Crisp on his similar machine.

Two years later, speedway and stock car promoter Mike Parker, who had helped launched speedway at Newport (see Chapter Three), became involved, with plans for monthly long-track meetings on Thursday evenings, and more frequent Friday and Saturday events for cars. However, complaints from nearby residents prompted Prestatyn Urban Council to ask the High Court to ban motor sport at the venue. At

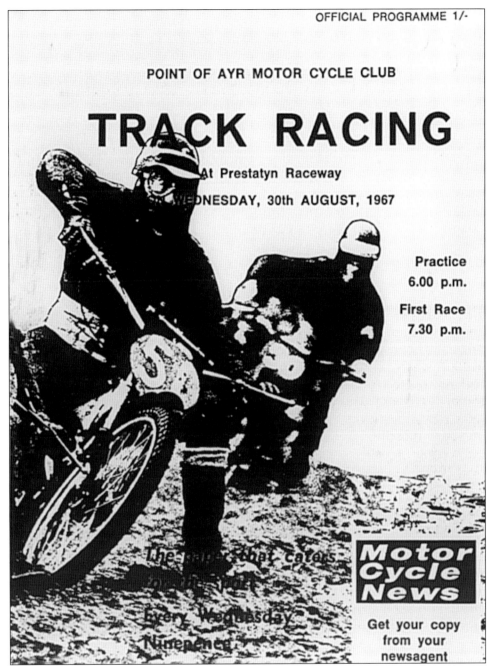

Prestatyn's first season of long track racing attracted some of the sport's top names. The 30 August 1967 meeting boasted an impressive line-up, with New Zealander Ivan Mauger winning the final race.

a hearing in July 1969, judge Mr Justice Goff refused the application. Although he accepted there might be a nuisance, he said the council had given permission for racing and could not then obtain an order to stop it. He suggested the council's action might have been motivated by its concern about negotiations with the Pontins company for the development of a neighbouring site as a holiday village. However, he did rule that there could be no playing of music over loudspeakers between races.

Rhyl-based Vic Lonsdale, Australian John Boulger and Dave Baybutt were among the top performers at the venue in 1968 and '69, and the track continued to draw some of the sport's biggest names. The meeting on 29 May 1969, for instance, lived up to its billing as the 'Clash of the Champions', with an impressive entry list. This included Wolverhampton Wolves' England internationals Norman Hunter and James Bond, New Zealand's four-times world champion Barry Briggs, rising Belle Vue star Chris Pusey, Don Godden and veteran Lew Coffin.

However, the world class entries did not impress everyone and, later that year, local hoteliers went to court to stop the racing because of noise, vibration and dust. Their lawyer told the hearing that the track had originally been used for trotting. He described it as 'a rather sedate form of sport' and this was contrasted with the bike and car racing, which was apparently advertised as involving 'hell drivers' and 'men who scream round the track.' The raceway was located in a 'good class residential area,' the court was told. Racing was ultimately curtailed, although Prestatyn remained a popular venue for horse-power of a different kind – the more 'sedate' sport of trotting continuing as a popular attraction long after the engines had been silenced.

More recently, Graham Drury, promoter of the popular ice speedway events at Telford, expressed an interest in running long-track racing on the trotting track at the neighbouring coastal resort of Rhyl. However, in March 2002, he had reluctantly given up on the idea because the uncertainties of the weather made the huge investment too risky. He said his plan was to stage a major event with top riders, but the cost made it too much of a gamble. He was, however, willing to help anyone interested in putting on such an event. So long-track racing may yet return to Wales.

Ammanford

Wales's second long-track venue was more short-lived and much more low-key than the Prestatyn venture. The track known as Ammanford was actually some miles away on the Ty-Gwaith pony-trotting track, near Brynamman. Carmarthen Motorcycle Club leased the half-mile track

Ammanford's only long track event, in 1970, was effectively a grass-track meeting on a cinder speedway.

from the owners, Bryn Llewellyn and Eifion Jones, for a one-off motor-cycle meeting on Sunday 12 September 1970.

The meeting was very much a grass-track event relocated on to a cinder speedway, and the entry – mainly from grass-track – reflected that. However, riders travelled from the far corners of England to join some enthusiastic locals. One of those visitors, Tig Perry, an experienced grasser from the West Country, took the honours in the main 500cc solo competition, as well as the 250cc class, while the unlimited class went to I. Lawrence from Kidderminster. The meeting also featured sidecars, with G. Lloyd of Rugby winning two of the events and G. Hancox of Leamington Spa the other.

The track, with its long, flat bends, sixty to eighty feet wide, never hosted the bikes again, and it would be more than thirty years before speedway returned to West Wales with the opening of the Carmarthen track in 2002 (see Chapter Five).

5

CARMARTHEN

Speedway's newest Welsh home is Carmarthen in south-west Wales. The town's team was launched in 2002, joining Newport Mavericks as a second Welsh side in the Conference League. Following the patriotic example of Cardiff, Neath and briefly Newport, they adopted the name Dragons.

Efforts had been made to introduce speedway to Carmarthen more than thirty years before, when Swansea businessman Peter Atkinson put on a demonstration. However, local officials were unimpressed, as a rider was thrown over the barrier into the spectator area. Grass track racing was held in the town in 1939 and 1946. More recently, in 1986, Dave Perry won the 500cc event at Carmarthen Park on a track surrounding the Carmarthen Athletic rugby pitch. The meeting on 10 June was described as a kind of muddy speedway event, with seven riders in each race on a track of approximately 400 metres.

Real speedway arrived in April 2002, with Carmarthen Dragons opening their Conference League campaign with an historic all-Wales clash at Newport. The match on Easter Monday, 1 April, marked the first league encounter between two Welsh teams in the history of the sport, and it was a successful debut for the West Walians. Carmarthen came from behind to win 46-43 in an eventful meeting at Hayley Stadium. In the first heat, former Maverick David Gough broke the tapes and was handicapped fifteen yards for the restart. When they got under way again, Newport's Simon Walker fell, forcing Gough to lay down his bike to avoid him. Gough failed to finish the second restart, which saw Dean Felton register Dragons' first points when he finished second behind Mavericks' Scott Pegler. Carmarthen's first race winner was Shane Colvin, who picked up the three points in heat three. Darren Pugh – a former grass-track rider in his first season of speedway – recovered from a bad fall in heat four to win the eighth race. With Gough grabbing second just before the line, Dragons scored a 5-1 heat win which put them into a lead they would never give up.

Speedway was brought to Carmarthen by father and son Nigel and Gordon Meakins, joint chairmen of the club, with Nigel doubling up as team manager and Gordon as one of the team's key riders. Before that

The Carmarthen Dragons of 2002. From left to right, back row: Gordon Meakins, Tristan Brewer, David Gough, Craig Taylor. Front row: Shane Colvin, Dean Felton, Darren Pugh.

Shane Colvin on his way to becoming Carmarthen's first race winner in the league. Here he leads Newport's Rob Finlow (right) and Jamie Holmes.

league debut, a four-man Carmarthen team rode in a six heat exhibition match in Somerset, against a Somerset Rebels B team, on 12 October 2001. Dragons, represented by Meakins, Tristan Brewer, Brendan McKay and Gerry Simms, won 24-12.

Dragons' first home match took place on 21 April 2002 on a purpose-built track within the county showground on the edge of town. Nigel had attended his first speedway meeting at Oxford at the age of nine and went on to ride at Swindon and Reading in the late 1960s, but his speedway career ended with a serious arm injury at Kings Lynn. His son, Gordon, rode as a schoolboy, but when the family moved to Carmarthenshire, any involvement in speedway seemed to have ended for good. However, Gordon took up grass-track racing in the late 1980s, and soon found speedway was beckoning again. 'We kept going

Craig Taylor leads Newport's Jamie Holmes during the opening league clash on 1 April 2002.

Gordon Meakins ahead of Somerset's Tim Healy during the four-a-side challenge on 12 October 2001. Dragons won 24-12.

past the showground and thinking that would make a good place for a speedway,' Nigel recalled. It was literally a case of not having a track nearby, so deciding to build one. The circuit was constructed throughout the winter of 2001 to 2002 on a tight budget, financed by re-mortgaging the house. The council gave permission for 14 home matches in Dragons' inaugural season, and the season began with the Meakins hoping to enthuse the rugby-loving West Wales public with a new sport.

6

THE WELSH WORLD CHAMPION

Without doubt the greatest speedway rider to come out of Wales was Fred Williams. His World Championship victories in 1950 and 1953 made him the first Briton to take the title twice, and for good measure he was runner-up in 1952. Williams never rode for a Welsh team, but made his name with the great Wembley Lions and rode for England in test matches around the world.

Born in Port Talbot in 1926, the Second World War took Williams away from home to the south coast of England, where he worked as an engine-fitter in the naval dockyards in Portsmouth. At the weekends, he would often return home to South Wales, where he rode in grass-track events. He had trials at Rye House, where Wembley boss Alec Jackson spotted his talent and gave him the chance of a speedway career. That career was put on hold, however, after a grass-track accident left him with a fractured ankle and torn ligaments, which kept him sidelined for five months.

He made his debut on 23 October 1947 against Odsal Boomerangs, collecting a point from his two rides. He impressed sufficiently to be regarded as the first-choice reserve for 1948. Injuries to captain Bill Kitchen and George Wilks opened up an opportunity for Williams to take a regular place in the side. He rode in 24 matches and scored 125 points – an average of 5.21 – in a Wembley team which had to run most of its home matches at Wimbledon, while the Empire Stadium was used for the Olympic Games. He improved on that in 1949, with 232 points and an average of 6.44, helping Lions to a third post-war National League title, and earning himself a call-up into the England team – despite being a fiercely proud Welshman.

For 1950, Williams was the mainstay of the Wembley team, and his younger brother Eric was making his way into the side. Lions won the league title again, as Freddie's average moved up to 8.18. He also helped England to a 3-2 Ashes series win against Australia, but his place in the record books was earned by his performance in the world championship. His campaign started poorly with a six-point haul at Belle Vue in

Fred Williams – Wales's double world champion.

August. However, a more useful 13 from the Wembley round and 14 from West Ham gave him a total of 33 and seventh place in the top 16 – which meant a place in the final at his home track. In the first heat, Williams finished ahead of West Ham's Wally Green – whose runner-up spot in the championship would be as big a surprise as Williams' win. Next came victory over Split Waterman, Vic Duggan and Danny Dunton, and in his third outing Jack Young and Graham Warren were among the victims.

His only defeat came in his next race, when Jack Parker nipped through on the inside as Williams was battling Aub Lawson for the lead. In his final appearance, he finished ahead of rising New Zealand star Ronnie Moore and defending champion Tommy Price. With 14 points to his credit, Williams was the world champion, and a civic reception awaited him in his home town, as well as invitations to race in Sweden and Denmark.

The next year, he helped Wembley to another league crown, with a further improved average of 9.0, while brother Eric continued to improve, with an average of 6.09. In the test matches against Australia, Freddie led the scoring for England with 11 points at Harringay and 13 in the home side's only win of the series at Bradford. He scored 12 in the third test at Wembley, though Split Waterman outscored him here with 13. Although Williams qualified for the world final, defending his title always looked likely to be struggle for the Welshman in 1951. He won his first heat, but finished third in the next, and then came home last in his third race to end any hopes of the crown.

In 1952, Wembley won the National League title yet again, with Williams scoring 334 points from 36 matches for an improved average of 9.2, which sent him up to fourth in the rider rankings. He qualified well for the world final and beat the much-fancied Ronnie Moore in his

A cartoon showing Fred Williams leading the British assault on Australia in 1949.

International action – Williams leads the pack at Randfontein, South Africa in 1954.

opening heat, but West Ham's Australian Jack Young established a points lead which would ensure he retained his title. However, a win in his last outing would give Williams the runner-up spot. He finished ahead of Arthur Forrest, Graham Warren and Dick Bradley to finish behind Young in the championship.

Although the Coronation year, 1953, saw the demise of Cardiff Dragons down in the Southern League (see Chapter One), it brought more success for the Welsh speedway star in exile. Williams' Wembley won the National League title yet again. It was their seventh championship in the eight post-war seasons, and – as it turned out – their last, with Wimbledon soon to emerge as the new London-based force in British speedway. The Welshman reached the world final again, and overcame hot favourite Young, to win a second championship. Williams dropped only one point all night, to Harringay captain Jeff Lloyd.

His victory owed much to his grass-track experience and his continuing dedication to practice. Heavy rain had made the Wembley track too slippery for many to manage, but Freddie's early days on the tricky grass courses had given him the ability to cope with the unpredictable surface. He also revealed that during the season, he had carried out almost 1,000 practice starts in the Wembley car park. Starting proved vital on the big night, the Welshman beating the rest to the first bend in four of his five races. That included the vital heat 17, when he faced the previously unbeaten Split Waterman, Sweden's Olle Nygren and Australian Aub Lawson – all of whom still had a chance of the title at that stage. Williams won the race to beat Waterman to the Championship by a single point, and he received the trophy from Everest conquerors Sir Edmund Hillary and Sir John Hunt.

A month later, Williams married Olympic ice skater Pat Devries and their honeymoon in South Africa was combined with Freddie's duties as a member of the touring England team. The world champion became an instant star on the South African scene, and was one of the big international names who boosted the sides in the country's inter-province matches during the mid-1950s.

Back in Britain, he maintained his position among the league's top performers. In 1954, his 240 points from 28 matches gave him an average of 8.57, and although his form slipped next season, he scored a further maximum at West Ham on 21 June 1955. His riding career ended after the first ten matches of 1956, with an average of 3.8, but he went on to manage the Wembley team during their 1970s revival.

FOOTNOTE

Speedway historian Peter Jackson has produced modern style statistics for riders from the 'golden era' by analysing the results of all Division One matches and adding bonus points – a concept not widely recognised in those days, but now routinely included in rider statistics.

With Peter Jackson's permission, below are Freddie Williams' modern-style Division One statistics, including his CMA or calculated match average.

Season	Matches	Actual points	Bonus Points	Total	CMA	Ranking
1947	1	1	0	1	2	-
1948	24	125	25	150	6.38	33rd
1949	35	232	27	259	7.40	25th
1950	32	263	17	280	8.75	13th
1951	31	279	21	300	9.76	3rd
1952	36	333	12	345	9.65	3rd
1953	16	161	4	165	10.31	4th
1954	28	240	17	257	9.18	10th
1955	24	183	11	194	8.43	24th
1956	10	38	7	45	5.14	44th

Corporate hospitality and advertising packages are part of the modern speedway scene – as this publicity material from Newport Wasps shows.

Wales has featured only rarely in international competition. This programme is from a 1964 tournament at Exeter, where a four-man 'Wales' team from Newport Wasps finished third behind Scotland and England, but ahead of the Overseas quartet.

TRACK LIST

Speedway and long-track venues in Wales

The table below lists the venues in Wales which have staged speedway or long-track racing. It does not include temporary grass or sand-racing tracks.

Town/City	Venue	Years of operation
Cardiff	White City	1928-1937
Pontypridd	Taff Vale Park	1929
Tredegar	Recreation Ground	1929-1930
Caerphilly	Virginia Park	1931-1932
Cardiff	Penarth Road	1951-1953
Neath	Abbey Stadium	1962
Newport	Somerton Park	1964-1977
Prestatyn	Prestatyn Raceway*	1967-1969
Ammanford	Ty-Gwaith*	1970
Newport	Hayley Stadium	1997-present
Cardiff	Millennium Stadium	2001-present
Carmarthen	United Counties Showground	2002-present

*indicates long track

UPDATE

Speedway is a fast-moving sport off the track as well as on it. So much so, that even in the few months between submitting the text of this book and its preparation for publishing, much has happened that warrants inclusion in this potted history of the sport in Wales.

The biggest event, of course, was the 2002 British Grand Prix at Cardiff's Millennium Stadium on 8 June. Although talk of a capacity crowd in the huge arena (see chapter one) turned out, predictably, to be nothing more than talk, an estimated 40,000 attended the summer spectacular – a significant increase on the first Cardiff GP the previous year. The streets of the Welsh capital were taken over by speedway fans from far and wide, and the build-up was aided by the presence of an all-day speedway collectors' fair in a nearby hotel.

On the track, there were surprises galore, as many of the top riders failed to reach the final. The meeting ran very late, thanks to no fewer than ten re-runs, and there was concern among some aficionados that the surface was too slippery and the inside gate had an unfair advantage. However, the track held up better than it had the previous year, with no ruts developing, and overall the event was seen as an improvement on the hugely successful 2001 meeting.

Some of the established favourites would have disagreed, however. They fell (sometimes literally) by the wayside, as three Australians and a Swede made it to the final – none of them having won a Grand Prix previously. Reigning Champion, and winner in Cardiff the previous year, Tony Rickardsson demanded a re-run after he was eliminated at the semi-final stage, claiming the start light had not been working, but his plea was rejected. So Mikael Karlsson was the only European in the last four, but it turned into a battle of the Australians. Todd Wiltshire took an early lead, but Ryan Sullivan came round the outside to pass his compatriot and take the chequered flag. Once again, the magnificent venue was a talking point after the meeting. Commenting on his victory, Sullivan said: 'It hasn't sunk in yet – this is what I have been dreaming about, and what a place to do it. The atmosphere here today was incredible but I tried to keep it out of my mind.'

The 2002 Welsh Open Championship at Newport on 9 June, the day after the Grand Prix, was delayed by an hour because of heavy rain. When it finally got underway, Newcastle's Andre Compton emerged as the winner. Denmark's Jesper Jensen took second place – on his first appearance at Hayley Stadium – while another finalist, Ipswich's Craig Boyce, had to be taken to hospital, with mild concussion and a shoulder injury.

In mid-June, Wales' Premier League team, Newport Wasps were eleventh in the seventeen-team table, with three wins and a draw from their eight matches. Australians Craig Watson and Frank Smart had made triumphant returns, and were helping to lift the side out of the doldrums of the previous year.

The season was marred, however, by a serious accident at Newport in April, when former Wasp Lawrence Hare, riding for Exeter Falcons, suffered neck and back injuries during the Devon team's visit to Wales. The thirty-two-year-old was left paralysed and was told it is unlikely that he will walk again. After eight weeks in the Royal Gwent Hospital, Hare was able to get out for the first time on 8 June, to attend the Cardiff Grand Prix.

In the Conference League, Carmarthen Dragons suffered early season injury troubles, with Graig Gough ruled out for the season and captain Craig Taylor temporarily sidelined. However, the new side was still in the top half of the table in mid-June. Newport Mavericks had an unhappier start to the 2002 campaign, with a single win from their first five matches.

Andrew Weltch
June 2002

AUSSIE RULES
Sullivan pulls off surprise British Grand

AUSTRALIAN Ryan Sullivan has upset the form book and put himself at the top of the Speedway Grand Prix Series after a fantastic victory in Cardiff last night.

Sullivan was one of three Aussies in the final after hot favourite Tony Rickardsson went out in the semis.

Jason Crump and Thomasz Gollab, the Polish Grand Prix winner, also failed to make the final.

Rickardsson had previously been in fantastic form, winning his heats by almost the length of the rugby pitch which is usually in the centre of the stadium.

The Swede defeated world number two Jason Crump, from Australia, in ominous style to reach the semi-finals of last night's event.

And there was a shock in that heat which was virtually a re-run of the Polish Grand Prix final, when the winner of that event, Tomasz Gollab, finished last.

Earlier Britain's interest struggled to continue, with Mark Loram, who was third in Poland, finishing last in heat 19 behind Australian Ryan Sullivan, although the unexpected package of England's Lee Richardson did finish third in that heat.

However, Joe Screen was eliminated from the event in heat 17 which was won by American Billy Hamill.

The 30,000 crowd at the stadium were in raptures as the stars from across the world roared into life around them.

An enormous amount were from Britain, with the flag of St George and Union Jacks being as prevalent as they were in the Far East on Friday for England's World Cup match with Argentina.

Earlier, Britain lost a couple of riders in Workington's Carl Stonehewer, who was eliminated in the pre-main event, as well as Andy Smith, who was also eliminated before the later stages.

However, Crump, the grandson of Newport Wasps team manager Neil Street and son of former Wasp Phil Crump, was still on the charge to get on to the podium which he has missed out on agonisingly over the last events.

Crump finished fourth in Norway and also last in the Polish Grand Prix final.

Also out of the competition went Joe Screen, the Englishman who wears zebra leathers on his body and whose bike is also covered with zebra motifs.

Earlier the massive crowd at the stadium was entertained by legendary rock singer Suzie Quatro, who did three numbers off her greatest hits amid a fireworks display, as the tension built up.

The riders were introduced to the crowd amid a smokescreen and unbelievable noise which could have been heard in Barry.

The roars of the engines greeted the start of the Grand Prix and it was not long before the heat built up, with the roars of the engines mixed with the petrol fumes which filled the Millennium Stadium.

It was a fantastic turnaround as well to make the stadium fit for a Grand Prix of this size after staging the Heineken European Cup final just a couple of weeks ago.

That rugby match was awesome because of the noise it generated, but speedway fans proved that they can be as noisy as other sports last night.

SWEDE DREAMS
Mikael Karlasson of Sweden leads Scott Nicholls during the speedway grand prix *Picture: David Davies*

Making the headlines: the 2002 Grand Prix again brought speedway to the attention of the Welsh media. This impressive two-page spread appeared in Wales on Sunday *within hours of the event.*

SPEEDWAY!
Prix victory in front of thousands

AUSSIE RULES Number eight, Todd Wiltshire from Australia leads the riders during the first corner of the FIM Egg British Speedway Grand Prix at the Millennium Stadium *Picture: David Davies*